D1013256

WHITNEY
HOUSTON

WHITNEY HOUSTON

THE VOICE, THE MUSIC, THE INSPIRATION

BY NARADA MICHAEL WALDEN

WITH RICHARD BUSKIN

FOREWORD BY CHAKA KHAN

INSIGHT  EDITIONS

San Rafael, California

This book is dedicated with love to Whitney's mom, Cissy, her daughter,

Bobbi Kristina, my mother, Marguerite "Peggy Hackley" Walden,

my father, Harold "Big H" William Walden, and Ron Walden,

the best brother and friend anyone could ever have.

CONTENTS

BY CHAKA KHAN

FIRST MET WHITNEY HOUSTON when she was still just a teenager. Her mother, Cissy, was my number-one background singer, and during a 1979 recording session for my second solo album, *Naughty*, she told me, "I have a daughter who sings."

"Really?" I asked. "How old is she?"

"Sixteen," Cissy replied.

"Well, bring her down here," I said. "We can sing some stuff together!"

That's what happened. When Whitney showed up with Cissy the next day, I was working on "Clouds," which, like my hit recording of "I'm Every Woman" the year before, was produced by Arif Mardin and written by the husband-and-wife team of Nickolas Ashford and Valerie Simpson. It was Whitney's first studio session, and I was really knocked out by how well she sang backup. "Wow, a star is born!" I recall telling her and Cissy. It was clear that Whitney had a special talent.

Throughout the years, after her own career took off, we would occasionally run into each other when we were performing in the same city or perhaps attending the same awards show, and Whitney was always like a little sister to me. However, being that we were both so busy, we didn't get all that many opportunities to hang out together. One of the best came in late 1992, when Whitney asked me to make a cameo appearance in the video to promote her cover of "I'm Every Woman." She did a great job with that song, and we had a really beautiful time during the filming.

As a singer, Whitney was one of the absolute best. Not only was she blessed vocally, but she also had great communication skills—whenever she sang something, it was totally believable, and we could always feel the emotion she was trying to convey: love, joy, sadness, you name it. In addition to her daughter, Bobbi Kristina, Whitney's legacy is her music, and that's why I'm so glad Narada Michael Walden has now written this book about her.

I've been involved in several different projects with Narada down the years, and he's not only a great artist but also a lovely man who, within these pages, recalls his fascinating experiences collaborating with one of the greatest vocalists of our time on many of her finest records. This is really important because with Whitney, it was all about the music, and Narada is writing about the main thing for which she'd want to be remembered—her body of work—which will last for all time.

Although spiritually transformed—and despite the fact that I miss hearing her voice, admiring her beauty, and being enchanted by her warmth, intelligence, and sharp sense of humor—Whitney is still around and always will be. Now that she has graduated from this realm, we should celebrate her life, and one of the best ways to do this is to listen to her records and, by reading on, learning how they came to be.

FOR THE LOVE
OF WHITNEY

THAT VOICE. HER VOICE. *What* a voice. A voice that seamlessly blended angelic sweetness with raw power, richness with intensity, soul and gospel with pop and R&B. A voice of tremendous range, control, and dexterity that made the belting of high notes sound effortless while infusing the most tender love songs with an alluring warmth. A voice with a quick vibrato—almost imperceptible to those who heard her sing in the studio—that embellished every number with an innate, infectious energy. And a voice whose owner had that rare ability to shift it into a fifth gear, displaying its most stunning qualities by digging deep to come up with moments of pure vocal inspiration.

When I worked with Whitney Houston between 1984 and 1993, producing many of the hits that now serve as part of her priceless musical legacy, she truly did have it all—not only as a singer but also as a smart, funny, compassionate woman whose striking physical beauty was matched by her inner strength and justifiable self-confidence. You see, Whitney loved the sound of her own voice. And those of us who had the privilege of hearing her up close fell in love with it, too—as well as with the alternately sensitive and mischievous creature affectionately called "Nippy" by her family and close friends, myself included.

Although the two of us grew up amid different surroundings—she in Newark and East Orange, New Jersey, me in Kalamazoo, Michigan—Whitney and I had several fundamental things in common. Okay, so being raised a Catholic didn't expose me to the kind of Baptist and Pentecostal churches where she sang exuberant, inspirational gospel hymns. But I was familiar with the sound emanating from the black churches on the north side of Kalamazoo, where the members' excitement, jubilation, and "We are One!" attitude characterized our joint devotion to God. "My Lord and Savior Jesus Christ," Whitney would repeatedly say (even in the middle of a recording session), referring to the Lord's constant presence in our daily lives. She was comfortable in the knowledge that this rang the same bell in me as it did in her, and I gained spiritual strength simply by being around her.

At the same time, having been influenced as a kid by everyone from Ray Charles, Smokey Robinson, and Julie London to Johnny Mathis, Dusty Springfield, and Dionne Warwick—while also loving the songs of Burt Bacharach and Hal David—I had a strong musical bond with Whitney. After all, c'mon—the cousin of Dionne, daughter of Cissy Houston, goddaughter of Darlene Love, and honorary niece of Aretha Franklin? That girl's blue-blooded connections spoke to my musical soul, as did her love of Roberta Flack, Gladys Knight, and Chaka Khan. Not for nothing did we have such an incredible rapport in the studio.

So, why am I writing this book? Well, when I attended Whitney's funeral service on February 18, 2012, I was not only touched to see all of the flowers that people had sent, but I was also deeply moved by the thousands of fans who—despite having no chance of being allowed inside Newark's New Hope Baptist Church—showed up because of their love for her. Being a fan myself, I immediately wanted those who love Whitney to know more about her: to know how kind and caring she was, how much fun she was to be around, and what she gave of herself to make timeless hit records. The only artist to have seven consecutive U.S. chart-topping singles, Whitney was, according to the *Guinness World Records*, the most awarded female act of all time.

The negative aspects of her later years aren't a part of this story—I wasn't around to witness them and they've already received more than enough tabloid coverage. Instead, I'm writing about the Whitney *I* knew, recalling the things *she* would want me to share, in the hope that readers will not only be informed and entertained by what went on behind the scenes but that they will also be inspired by her efforts and achievements. For me, music is the supreme language of a higher force, and Whitney was a master of that language, right up there with all the greats.

The body of work that she left behind needs to be understood within its proper context, and I'm just so grateful that I can contribute to that effort (having, as you will soon read, nearly passed up the opportunity to collaborate with her before Divine Will intervened). The great team of Clive Davis and Arista Records, Whitney's mom and dad, her close friends including Robyn Crawford—all of us were firsthand witnesses to Whitney's genius, as well as to the creative explosion that launched her career into the stratosphere. Now, while we're still mourning her loss, I'm happy to recount my memories of the very honest and vulnerable person— the *real* person—I was lucky to know.

This book is for the love of Whitney—my Nippy!

—Narada Michael Walden
San Rafael, California

"When I first laid eyes on Whitney at the session for 'How Will I Know,' she was drop-dead gorgeous. In the studio, I asked her to run through the track so I could get a sound balance on her voice, but when I returned to the control room, Narada said, 'Mike, this is not going to be a run-through. Whatever you do, make sure you capture her voice because I have a feeling she's gonna sing it once and that'll be it.' Narada hadn't worked with her before, but he's otherworldly—he was tuned in and I was going with what he said. So, over the talkback I asked Whitney if she was ready for the run-through, she said she was, and, without telling her, I pressed RECORD on the tape machine. Once she began singing it was hard for me to believe what I was hearing. Not only did she have a spectacular voice, but it blended so perfectly with the music and backing vocals that it was like listening to the finished record. I had to keep looking at her through the control room window to believe this was actually happening. When Whitney finished her 'run-through,' she said, 'Okay, I'm ready to do it for real,' to which Narada replied, 'Honey, you just did.'"

—MICHAEL BARBIERO, recording engineer

CHAPTER ONE

A 400-LB. GIRL
IN A 100-LB. BODY

THE FIRST TIME I WORKED with Whitney she blew me
away. It was October 1984, we were at Mediasound in
downtown Manhattan to capture her vocal for "How
Will I Know," and before she even sang a note I was
both captivated and humbled by the twenty-one-year-old's stunning looks and personal aura. Then, when she opened her mouth
and that dynamic sound poured out of the control-room speakers,
I was floored by the power of her voice and the poise with which
she handled it. Damn, this baby sister was something else!

Whitney originally learned to play the piano while performing as a soloist in Newark's New Hope Baptist Church junior
gospel choir, debuting there at the age of eleven with a heartfelt
rendition of the popular Welsh hymn "Guide Me, O Thou Great
Jehovah." Only a year earlier, as a struggling twenty-one-year-old

drummer, I had become a follower of the Bengali spiritual teacher Sri Chinmoy. About six months later, I joined the Mahavishnu Orchestra of fellow disciple and guitarist Mahavishnu John McLaughlin, a pioneer in the fusion of jazz, rock, and Indian classical music. Therefore, although separated by age and geographical distance, Whitney and I had been traveling along parallel, spiritually inspired musical paths.

A cousin of opera diva Leontyne Price, Nippy's mother, Cissy, sang backup for the likes of Elvis Presley, Jimi Hendrix, Otis Redding, Aretha Franklin, Dionne Warwick, Bette Midler, Van Morrison, and Mahalia Jackson, In 1979, she also scored her own Top 40 disco hit with "Think It Over." Which is why, in addition to absorbing the music she heard in church, at home, on the radio, and at some of Cissy's recording sessions, Nippy had benefited from regular vocal coaching by her mom. Talk about an incredible musical education—the two of them had even sung onstage together at some of the nightclubs where Cissy performed.

Their song repertoire had included "Ain't No Way," which Aretha had recorded in 1968 with Cissy singing backup, and Barbra Streisand's "Evergreen," on which Whitney handled the lead. Believe me, this would have never happened if she hadn't already convinced her mom that she possessed serious talent, and this had been borne out when, at the tender age of fourteen, she sang backup on the Michael Zager Band's "Life's a Party."

What followed in her teen years was a period when Whitney honed her craft via every performance opportunity that came her way, and in 1980 Zager actually offered her a record deal that Cissy rejected because her daughter was still in high school. On the other hand, after the kid had caught a photographer's eye during an early-'80s Carnegie Hall stage appearance with her mom, Cissy had approved of Whitney raising her profile and earning good money as a part-time fashion model because she could do so without interrupting her studies.

That camera guy saw what I and everyone else saw—true beauty and irresistible charm—and within no time Nippy became one of the first women of color to appear on the cover of *Seventeen* magazine, while also being featured in the pages of such top publications as *Cosmopolitan* and in a TV ad for Canada Dry. Then, once she completed high school, her ongoing live performances and lead vocal on a cover of the Soft Machine song "Memories" for the 1982 Material album *One Down* started to attract an increasing amount of industry attention.

After Arista A&R exec Gerry Griffith saw Whitney perform at a Manhattan club named Seventh Avenue South—and been floored by her rendition of "Tomorrow" from the stage musical *Annie*—he'd arranged a showcase for her at New York's Top Cat Studio and persuaded Clive Davis to attend. Knocked out by not only Whitney's soaring vocal range and lyrical expressiveness but also her natural poise and personal charm, Clive then fought off competition from Elektra to sign the breathtaking nineteen-year-old to her first, worldwide record deal and set about assembling the right material and producers for her debut album.

"She was that rare combination of the stunning beauty of Lena Horne with the gospel fire and strength of Aretha Franklin," he'd later tell an interviewer for A&E's *Biography*. Nevertheless, as Clive had also been well aware, "A great artist with a great voice that looks good does not sell without great songs. In the case of Whitney, for two years she and I prepared for showcases where I invited the best writers and producers in America to say, 'Give me your great songs because this artist is going to be special.'"

While this was taking place, Whitney recorded "Eternal Love" for the 1983 LP *Paul Jabara & Friends*, duetted with Arista stablemate Jermaine Jackson on a number titled "Take Good Care of My Heart" from his 1984 *Dynamite* album, and did the same with Teddy Pendergrass on a sweet soul ballad called "Hold Me." Initially included on Teddy's *Love Language* album, this track was released as a single (during a pre-iTunes era when songs deemed to have commercial potential were often issued as separate entities on vinyl, cassette tape, and, a little later, on CD). It cracked the Top 50 on both sides of the Atlantic before being added to Nippy's inaugural, self-titled record. As you can see, by the time I began working with her, she was hardly an inexperienced novice.

Thankfully, I had already earned my stripes—drumming with the Mahavishnu Orchestra as well as on records by anyone from Rick James and Jeff Beck to Chick Corea and Carlos Santana, while composing material for Herbie Hancock and touring with Patti LaBelle. Also, in addition to releasing seven of my own albums, I had produced records by Don Cherry, Stacy Lattisaw, Sister Sledge, Patti Austin, and, of course, Miss Aretha Franklin.

All of this made me no stranger to working with artists of immense, sometimes legendary talent. Yet, until Whitney walked into Mediasound that day in October 1984 and proceeded to nail "How Will I Know," I had never encountered such an exceptional new singer who was so calmly and sweetly self-assured about her own abilities. That priceless combination is what made her an unstoppable force.

Whitney had edge in her sound. Whitney had edge in her voice. Whitney had edge in her character. You couldn't fool her. The first time she looked at you, you had to lay down. "I'm just so happy to be here in *your* presence" is how I'd feel. Forget that I was producing a relative newcomer. Swiftly, subtly, there had been a shift in power, achieved effortlessly and without causing any friction.

This kid had come a long way during the eight years since I'd first met her. Back in 1976, when the esteemed Tom Dowd co-produced my debut album, *Garden of Love Light*, he had suggested having Cissy Houston sing the title track. As far I knew, Cissy was mainly a backing singer. But the fact that Tom recommended her was good enough for me, and she subsequently arrived at New York's Atlantic Records studio in the company of three hot chicks and a little girl—an exquisite angel who didn't sing on the session but sat quietly in the corner.

No one introduced me to Cissy's adorable thirteen-year-old daughter, but her super-warm eyes, high cheekbones, and radiant smile had certainly piqued my curiosity. At least, until the session ended, at which point we'd gone our separate ways, and I had, quite honestly, forgotten all about her. Now fast-forward to the call I received from Arista's Gerry Griffith in October 1984, while we were recording the backing track to Aretha's "Freeway of Love" at the Automatt, a state-of-the-art San Francisco studio where I had done a ton of work.

"You know this girl named Whitney Houston?" Gerry asked me.

"No," I replied, bugged that I had to interrupt an important session to chat with a record company honcho about some unknown artist.

"Cissy's daughter, Whitney," Gerry continued.

"Oh, yeah, yeah, I met her one time, but that was years ago."

"Well, we just signed her."

"That's nice."

"I have a song I'd like you to produce for her."

"Yeah, but I haven't got the time to do anything else right now," I responded. "I'm tied up with Aretha on a *very* important mission."

"Then *make* the time," Gerry insisted.

Several people had already been recruited to produce tracks for Whitney's debut album—Jermaine Jackson, Kashif, Michael Masser—and Gerry thought that, given the up-tempo, dance-oriented work I had been doing with Aretha, I'd be ideally suited to take charge of a pop-crossover song that would contrast perfectly with the record's collection of ballads and R&B numbers. "How Will I Know" had been written for Janet Jackson by keyboardist George Merrill and singer Shannon Rubicam—the members of synthpop duo Boy Meets Girl—and, as I'd learn, they were pretty upset when her management turned it down on the grounds that it was weaker than the other material chosen for her third album, *Control.*

Janet's loss would be Whitney's gain, but that didn't happen right away. Gerry loved "How Will I Know" after the songwriters' publisher played him their demo, and Clive was quick to second that emotion. Not me, however. As soon as I heard it over the phone, I noted that the song had a strong chorus and nice bridge, but the verses were incomplete.

"Listen, I'm not even going to mess with this unless I can rewrite the sucker," I told Gerry, half-hoping he'd tell me to forget it so that I could get on with producing "Freeway of Love." Gerry, however, was nothing if not persistent.

"Okay, then let me call the writers and see if they'll agree to this," he said, much to my annoyance. Hell, this cat wouldn't let me go! We ended the conversation, and about ten minutes later Gerry called back to say that they were cool with me revising their composition. At that point, I had to accept I'd been boxed into a corner that was largely of my own making. Then again, I also knew it was meant to be because in this business things normally don't move that fast.

On the same day that I received the call from Gerry, I rewrote "How Will I Know" by sitting at the Automatt's piano and crafting proper verses. I adapted music from the song's chorus to create a melody, which I presented to the musicians who were there to work with me on "Freeway of Love." They included Randy Jackson on bass, keyboardists Walter Afanasieff and Preston Glass, and Corrado Rustici playing synth guitar, while David Frazer engineered.

"Okay, guys," I announced. "We've got to learn this new song for a new artist."

The original demo featured a guide vocal by Shannon Rubicam to illustrate the kind of performance that would be required of Janet Jackson. This, however, was in a really high key, and as far as I was concerned, Whitney might not be able to handle it. "Can she sing that high?" I asked Gerry before cutting the backing track for a singer whose voice I had still never even heard. After all, the first line I was writing—the opening line—would contain one of the highest notes in the entire song: "There's a boy . . ."

"I don't know about that" was his helpful reply. "Here's her number . . . Give her a call."

So, that's what I did, hastily introducing myself before asking Whitney, "Do you sing as high as that woman on the demo?"

"Yeah, keep it like that."

"Are you *sure*? It's really high!"

"Yeah."

She was super-cool, sounding puzzled as to why I would even ask such a question.

"Okay," I remarked skeptically, as if to say, "You think you can do it? Hey, be my guest!"

What I didn't yet know was that Whitney had a five-octave vocal range. Still, taking her at her word, I cut the backing track at the Automatt, again on the same day that I'd been given the assignment and composed the verses, because Gerry wanted the finished song right away.

The whole feel of the track was *mean*. At that time, Prince exerted a major influence on all of us in terms of probing new drum sounds, so we combined the largeness of a Linn drum machine with the thickness of me playing drum pads to create a beat that had both edge and warmth. Meanwhile, having a live band in the studio meant everything had to move fast—"Play this." "Play that." "Okay, let's recut your part." Within an hour, we had the song. My backing singer, Kitty Beethoven, then added a guide vocal, and days later I was in New York to record Whitney at Mediasound.

As prearranged, after engineering wizard Michael Barbiero had set up a Neumann U87 microphone for her and was ready to roll tape, the first people to arrive at the studio were Cissy and the sibling trio of Julia, Maxine, and Oren Waters. They were there to record the backing vocals, and they blew through them in one take. We then rewound the tape, they doubled themselves, and in two takes and about six or seven minutes we were virtually done with the background vocals. All that would be added was Whitney's own backing for the magic blend. It was incredible.

Even though this session was diverting me from my big Aretha project, I didn't think about that as soon as Nippy walked in. Yes, she was beautiful, but the other thing that struck me was her natural disposition, the kind you'd associate with Bob Marley—so cool that, even if you were badass, you'd go along with her. Whitney commanded respect without being arrogant, without saying a word, and that's where the aura came in. Instantly, I could see why she was creating such a buzz.

Unlike certain other artists, including those who are new to the scene, Nippy made no demands. She just exuded calmness and affability. After we played the "How Will I Know" backing track for her, Whitney began to sing and lit up the entire place with her unexpected power. Given her looks and her voice, she was the complete package. So many elements came together so effortlessly, it was like the torch had been passed to Whitney by Cissy, Dionne, Darlene, and Aretha, and now she was the new champion who could go beyond all of them.

Listen to her sing the high intro to "How Will I Know"—"There's a *boy* . . ." That's what I first heard: that take, that voice. We didn't mess with it. The first take was the keeper. We could have recorded a few more and compiled the best parts of different performances, but I was so taken with what I initially heard that I didn't see the need. Among all of the songs that I'd work on with Whitney, this was one of the few that she knew in advance of us getting together in the studio. That's why it took shape so fast. Instead of laboring on it for the better part of a day—or even longer—we were done in a matter of minutes.

Whitney's voice could be smooth—she could imitate Dionne really well, with all the sweetness that encompassed—but she also had her momma's side to her, flashing chest-voice power like she was slapping you in the face. This beautiful, beautiful girl had the gut-bucket blues, and hearing that for the first time was a shock. I mean, you don't usually get that unless you're listening to some 400-pound woman. But here she was, a thin, spectacularly gorgeous, twenty-one-year-old model with bouncy hair, wearing a little tight sweater, little tight jeans, little tight boots, and capable of transitioning from the smooth to the raw within the space of a single vocal line. Out of the blue, I was producing a phenomenon.

Having worked with Aretha, I was less astonished by Whitney's ability than I was surprised by her *confidence* in what she could do. She was so relaxed about everything, especially when she sang. Aretha loved the sound of her own voice, but believe me, that's unusual in a singer because most vocalists are insecure beyond belief. Yet in that regard, the youthful Whitney was the same as the veteran Aretha. And *both* of them had the all-seeing eye.

When Whitney came into the control room and we listened to the playback of "How Will I Know," I was a little bit flabbergasted by how amazing it sounded, but she was not. Really impressed, I therefore had to act like I wasn't just to match her laid-back demeanor. She was looking at me and checking me out as if to say, "What's up? You don't know how I sound? You don't understand what I do?" The truth was, until that session I didn't—I had no idea about the kind of talent I was dealing with, and it was only thanks to the good Lord above that I found out. Left to my own devices, I would have never got involved in the first place.

After Whitney's work was finished, my friend Premik Russell Tubbs overdubbed tenor saxophone in the style of Clarence Clemons, who wasn't available. I wanted that raw, nasty-ass sax, I knew Premik could provide it, and that's what he did. The song was then ready for Michael Barbiero to mix. Still, at that point, there was no way I could have anticipated the international success of "How Will I Know" or that the *Whitney Houston* album, which spawned several other hit singles, would place her on the fast-track to musical immortality.

Throughout my career, I have worked with a lot of very talented artists with huge potential, yet they didn't have one vital thing that Whitney possessed: the big push of Clive Davis when he put his mack hand down. Yes, she was supremely gifted, but she also had Clive's support and the record company's vast financial resources to ensure her records were heard everywhere, every hour, on the hour. That's what Clive was famous for—hop in the car and "How Will I Know" was on the radio; hop anywhere else and there it was, too. Meanwhile, the young woman who benefited from all of this was, I quickly discovered, an intriguing blend of knowledgeable and naïve.

The first time Whitney and I hung out together was when we went to dinner the same day she tracked her "How Will I Know" vocal, accompanied by her best friend and assistant, Robyn Crawford. They'd met when, as sixteen-year-olds, they had summer jobs at a community center in East Orange, New Jersey, where Whitney grew up. Since then they had been inseparable, and as I'd soon appreciate, Robyn was a very positive influence on Nippy, a faithful companion on whom she could completely rely. And she did. Because, believe me, the Whitney who walked around Manhattan with us on that particular evening was totally different from the one I'd just been growing accustomed to in the studio.

No longer the self-assured artist who was quietly in control of her recording environment, she handed me the power once we were out on the street. Forget the all-seeing eye—Whitney was now so innocent and inexperienced, she didn't appear to have any notion of where we should go or what we should do.

"What do you wanna eat?"

"I'm not sure. You decide."

"Well, is there anything you might have a taste for?"

"I don't know."

"There's a pizza place around the corner. Wanna go there?"

"Sure."

Had Whitney been in the studio, she probably would have decided what to eat from where and, if asked, ordered everyone else's food, too. This other side of her that suddenly revealed itself therefore came as something of a shock, even though I found it endearing. Nippy was a complex character.

"I think we're going to do 'The Greatest Love of All,'" she told me over pizza, referring to the George Benson power ballad that Michael Masser and Linda Creed had written for the 1977 Muhammad Ali biopic *The Greatest*.

"Really?" I replied. "Why are you doing *that*?"

"Uh, well, Michael thinks we can do something new with it."

I was clueless. To me, it was a corny song, so I didn't understand why she'd want to record it. However, convinced by Michael Masser that it was perfectly suited to her vocal talents, Whitney pushed for the number to be included on her debut record. It would end up being a U.S. chart-topper—which just goes to show how wrong we can be when making assumptions without giving someone the chance to prove their point. As I was about to find out, it was hard to say no to Whitney. She knew she was a hot motor scooter, and whatever she wanted, she got.

"Let's keep in touch," I said as we were exiting the pizza joint. "Here's my phone number."

She didn't offer me her number, and I didn't ask for it—I didn't want her to think I was hitting on her. Hoping to collaborate with Whitney again, I was concerned she might think I was crossing the line. So, the evening ended on a similar note to the one on which the day had begun: with a swift role reversal that saw my supposedly elevated status being flipped on its head.

Between Nothingness and Eternity—that was the name of the last Mahavishnu Orchestra album before I joined John McLaughlin's jazz-rock outfit. And that's where I felt I existed being around Whitney Houston. One minute, I'd be in control of a situation, taking her under my wing; the next, I'd be deferring to her strong will and precocious wisdom. For sure, it was a mind-bender, but it was all part of the amazing journey that, unwittingly, I had just embarked upon, and pretty soon, in our separate ways, we'd both be soaring toward the stars.

"When I was still a young kid working with Narada, one of my jobs was to pick up the artists from the airport and bring them to the studio in my really old BMW 2002. It was so small, the artists often couldn't fit all of their bags in the trunk. Well, the first time she came to Tarpan, Whitney sat in that tiny car with her assistant, Robyn, and she was so sweet about it, we quickly became good friends. At one point, when she was recording her vocal for 'I Wanna Dance with Somebody,' she asked me to join her in the studio—she was so nice, grateful, generous, and cool with everything she was going through, that she was comfortable with me laying on the floor, looking up at her, and encouraging her as she sang. There I was, witnessing history. I'd never heard anyone sing with that much clarity, control, and sensitivity, as well as with all of the incredible dynamics. Not only was Whitney amazingly talented, but she also had the intelligence to know how to sing and how not to sing. Just by how he interacted with artists, Narada could get them to reach inside themselves and achieve greatness every time he crafted a vocal. And he also knew when to offer them guidance and when to just let them do their thing. Engineer Dave Frazer worked so fast to capture a performance, he and Narada were like the Dynamic Duo, and with his kindness, charm, intellect, and musicality, Narada was able to get performances out of Whitney that no one else had brought out of her before."

—GREG "GIGI" GONAWAY, drummer

CHAPTER TWO

BORN FOR THIS

A S THE 1980S REACHED the midway mark, a significant development on the music scene was the blending of different genres and the traversing of boundaries that, only a short time earlier, had been considered sacrosanct. The pairing of Earth, Wind & Fire's Philip Bailey with Genesis' Phil Collins on "Easy Lover" was a transatlantic smash. Meanwhile, the Grammy Award–winning "Freeway of Love," which I co-wrote with Jeffrey Cohen and was the leadoff single from Aretha Franklin's *Who's Zoomin' Who* album, turned out to be a huge U.S. rock/R&B crossover hit.

This, of course, was the track I was in the middle of producing when I received a call from Arista's Gerry Griffith, asking me to drop everything and work on the pop/R&B crossover song "How Will I Know" for a certain young woman from East Orange, New Jersey. Popular music was broadening its scope, and in 1985 it also rediscovered its conscience via the Live Aid and Farm Aid benefit concerts, in addition to charity singles like "We Are the World" and "That's What Friends Are For." Meanwhile, Madonna was enjoying chart success alongside Duran Duran, Tina Turner, Stevie Wonder, Simple Minds, and Dire Straits, whose *Brothers in Arms* became the first album to sell a million copies on CD. And, just as important, in 1985 the world was introduced to Whitney Houston.

To coincide with the March release of her self-titled debut album, a full-page ad that Arista placed in *Billboard* magazine announced: "The power. The emotion. The magnetism. The kind of talent that's going to blow you away." Listeners clearly agreed. *Rolling Stone* referred to Whitney as "one of the most exciting new voices in years," while the *New York Times* hailed the arrival of "an exceptional vocal talent."

Arista's strategy was right on the money. Clive Davis chose "You Give Good Love," an R&B ballad produced by Kashif Saleem, as the lead single in the United States so that Nippy would start off by establishing herself in the black marketplace. The fact that this song also crossed over to the pop market, hitting number three on the Billboard Hot 100, was a better-than-expected result that ignited sales of the album.

Up next was the jazzy soul ballad "Saving All My Love for You," which targeted adult-contemporary listeners. Written by Gerry Goffin and producer Michael Masser, this global hit was the first of Whitney's record-breaking seven consecutive chart-toppers in the United States.

All of which brings us back to "How Will I Know," a track that not only appealed to the dance crowd but also, following its November '85 release, was Whitney's fastest-rising number one and secured her first appearance on MTV. The colorful, bouncy video directed by Brian Grant provided her with the opportunity to show that she knew all the right moves, and due to the song's mainstream appeal, it was played in heavy rotation. This meant she was exposed to a much wider audience. Until then—in the wake of MTV being rightly criticized for airing too few videos by black, Latino, and other minority artists—no African-American female had managed that feat. She was a true trailblazer.

Following the success of "You Give Good Love," Whitney toured as the opening act for Luther Vandross and Jeffrey Osborne before headlining her own shows around the United States through the end of '85. Then, on March 8, 1986, just under a year after *Whitney Houston* had first been issued, the album finally sat atop the Billboard 200 chart, where it remained for fourteen weeks—on either side of a three-week spell when Van Halen's *5150* occupied pole position. Its sales outstripped all of 1986's other big sellers, including the *Miami Vice* soundtrack, Barbra Streisand's *The Broadway Album*, Madonna's *True Blue*, Boston's *Third Stage*, and Bruce Springsteen's *Live/1975–85*. When Whitney picked up two American Music Awards and a Best Pop Vocal Performance Grammy for "Saving All My Love for You," it was like the icing on the cake.

In July of that same year, Nippy kicked off her Greatest Love World Tour, which, over the course of the next four months, saw her wowing capacity audiences in amphitheaters, arenas, and convention centers all over North America, Europe, Japan, and Australia. The tour coincided with a nonstop whirl of media interviews aimed at sustaining Whitney's mind-blowing success. At the same time, determined to capitalize on this as quickly as possible, Clive immediately began selecting the material for her next record.

Intent on making a more pop-oriented album this time around in response to her broad sales demographic, and impressed by how fast we had worked together on "How Will I Know," the Arista boss initially asked me to produce five tracks on the new album: "I Wanna Dance with Somebody (Who Loves Me)," "Just the Lonely Talking Again," "For the Love of You," "Where Do Broken Hearts Go," and "I Know Him So Well."

During a meeting with Clive in his bungalow at the Beverly Hills Hotel, he played me demos of some of the songs. Then, after I agreed to produce them, I played him a demo of the Preston Glass composition "Love Is a Contact Sport." Clive is a shrewd and thoughtful guy who rarely behaves as if he's excited about anything, but even he was noticeably thrilled about the songs he was choosing for Whitney. After listening to "Love Is a Contact Sport," he said, "Okay, fine, let's add it to the list. "

By then, I had my own recording setup in San Rafael, California, just north of San Francisco. The studio had started life as a facility named Tres Virgos back in 1980, when musicians Robin Yeager, Allen Rice, and Mike Stevens owned it. (Their September birthdates gave rise to the "Three Virgos" appellation.) Joan Baez, Van Morrison, Mickey Hart, the Tubes, and Stewart Copeland were just some of the artists who had recorded there. In 1985, shortly after the Automatt had closed its doors—its final sessions being the ones that I produced for the backing tracks to "Freeway of Love" and "How Will I Know"—I purchased Tres Virgos.

This was a decade after my guru, Sri Chinmoy, had named me Narada, telling me it means *supreme musician*. "Narada's soul brings from Heaven to Earth light, delight, and compassion," he had explained, "and takes back to Heaven from Earth, Earth's sufferings." Now, he anointed my studio *Tarpan*, which appropriately translates as *satisfaction unparalleled*.

Originally designed by Chips Davis, Tarpan Studios utilized his famed Live End, Dead End (LEDE) acoustics to create a clear, natural sound for anyone sitting behind the Trident TSM console that I acquired from the Automatt. The fabulous Janice Lee, also from the Automatt, jumped on board as my technologically proficient, extremely adept studio manager, and the brilliant David Frazer became my in-house engineer. Among the first artists to benefit from their talents were Jermaine Stewart, Kenny G, and "The Big Man" Clarence Clemons. Everything was running smoothly by the time the second Whitney album rolled around. Which is why, far removed from the pressures and distractions of New York and L.A., Tarpan would serve as the ideal environment for her to record in.

Before Whitney arrived, we spent two to three weeks laying down the backing tracks to most of the songs. All were straightforward except for "I Wanna Dance with Somebody," written for Nippy by George Merrill and Shannon Rubicam (who had penned "How Will I Know"). Clive loved the song—as Shannon explained, it had less to do with bopping in a disco than doing the dance of life with a long-term partner. However, when I listened to the rough demo, I thought it sounded way too country for Whitney. It made me envision Olivia Newton-John performing at the rodeo—a very sweet, white-bread pop arrangement that didn't tap into Nippy's black soul.

If this was to be a dance number, it needed to be funky, it needed to be *dirty*, because it had to move the ghetto as well as the Onassis boat if we were going to create a hit that appealed to everybody. That meant I had to put on my ghetto hat—my street hat, my dance-club hat—to ensure we had the right ingredients in the gumbo.

Clive's really smart. "I Wanna Dance with Somebody" was a powerful song with a great chorus, and he knew right away that, if I did my thing and Whitney sang it, we could have a number one record on our hands. I just had to figure out how to incorporate the ghetto outhouse to make it stink a little more. As my mentor Quincy Jones once told me, "You want to have the outhouse bottom with the penthouse view," because you can sell almost anything when it has pretty instrumentation on top and wicked, smoking drums underneath.

The first thing that David Frazer and I did was record the intro for "I Wanna Dance with Somebody" with the handclaps, my Roland TR-808 bass drum, and Randy Jackson's one-finger synth bass. By funking things up, we immediately made the song more black. The big, bold, full-blown *whoosh* that followed—featuring synth guitar, synth percussion, electronic drums, and alto sax, in addition to synth horns overdubbed at the Record Plant in Sausalito—would tell everyone in the clubs, "Get on the dance floor *now*," especially when Whitney later added her time-to-party "Whoo!"

This was a completely new version of the song. I had local girl Kitty Beethoven record a guide vocal to help Nippy understand how it should go and then we were ready to roll. The only problem was Whitney's health. A severe bronchial infection had caused the cancellation of several Australian gigs toward the end of her world tour, and by the time she showed up at Tarpan in December 1986, she was totally exhausted.

As soon as I saw Whitney, her face betrayed the strain of constantly having new things to do and new people to be "on" for, to look great for, to sing brilliantly for. *Just let her catch her breath and slow things down*, I told myself. Instead of making suggestions, I asked Nippy which song *she'd* like to start with, and she said, "For the Love of You." She knew and loved this smooth Isley Brothers soul ballad, so there'd be no need for her to learn or study it.

The backing track that I'd already produced had my programmed drums, Randy's Moog synth, Corrado Rustici's rhythm-funk guitar synth, Preston playing synths and creating the bird sounds, and Raul Rekow of Santana playing the congas. Kenny G's Lyricon electronic alto sax would be overdubbed later. However, since Whitney stated up-front that she wanted to perform all of her own harmonies, I suggested we do the backing vocals first to ease the pressure.

After taking a quick break to grab some other clothes and get comfortable, Whitney returned to the studio to overdub twenty to thirty backing parts for the song. It was tedious work, but the sound was just like angels singing from the skies. Once she came into the control room and heard all of her harmonies blend together, the shackles were off, a spark of happiness replaced the sadness in her eyes, and she experienced an energy high to the nth power. This was magical new turf for Whitney—she'd never heard her voice stacked in that way, simulating what Michael Jackson did with Quincy Jones and engineer Bruce Swedien on numbers such as "Billie Jean" and "Beat It."

Again, we took a little break, and this time as we chitchatted I helped Nippy unwind by massaging her neck, her shoulders, her hands, and her feet. There was nothing sexual to any of this—from the beginning, we'd created a relationship based on work and friendship, with me assuming the role of the big brother who made her feel safe and at ease. Our conversation and the massage re-energized her, and Nippy was soon ready to spend another two hours capturing her "For the Love of You" lead vocal. It was as if she had been born to do this—to become one of the greatest recording stars of all time by diving back into the studio waters where magic can happen and experimentation rules the day.

Whitney stood next to the grand piano in the main studio when she sang. For this sultry track—as with others in the same vein—we burned candles and lowered the lights to help get her in the right mood. It was like saying, "Relax, kick off your shoes, nobody's watching. Are you ready to love me? I'm ready for *you*." She had so much power as a vocalist, but one of the biggest challenges was to bring out the actress in this twenty-three-year-old rising star, to get her to really *feel* what she was singing.

Familiar with the work of composers like Burt Bacharach and Hal David—especially the hit songs recorded by cousin Dionne—Whitney knew all about music's sensitive side while also understanding the hot funk of the street. It was a case of dialing in what we wanted. Before tracking a song like "For the Love of You," I'd therefore have her sing sensitive numbers, such as "Alfie" and "Walk On By," to put her in the appropriate frame of mind.

For my part, influenced by Bacharach's sophisticated, sculpted sound—most notably on Dionne's recordings of "Make It Easy on Yourself," "Here I Am," "You'll Never Get to Heaven," and "Any Old Time of the Day"—I applied elements of it to the work that I did with Whitney. This included the vocal phrasing that's staggered way behind the beat, elongating notes to give more meaning to the lyrics, and, on a song such as "For the Love of You," the loungy use of vibes to make it as sensual as a see-through nightie. Like her mom, Whitney had Aretha's grit, but she had a far stronger musical connection to Dionne.

As anyone who saw Whitney perform live during her peak years will tell you, she could show off her God-given talents with consummate ease and sound every bit as good as she did on her records. Nevertheless, in the studio, I'd have her sing each song in separate parts to create results that would last forever. That's the difference between a live performance and a studio recording. In concert, people heard Whitney's killer voice. In the studio, even though she was more than capable of singing a song beautifully all the way through, we might want to vary the choices on the verse and the chorus, and here or there we might also want to double her voice or add some harmonies.

Having a singer like Kitty Beethoven cut the guide vocal with all of the ad-libs and other elements was important because it served as the blueprint for Whitney and me. We did multiple takes of "For the Love of You" while trying new things as we went along. First, with eyes closed and a serene expression on her delicate, smooth-as-porcelain face, Nippy performed the final chorus because I wanted the church to come out and her spirit to sing. She did this without even warming up very much—she just hit it and killed it. She knew about the power of inspiration, and she didn't want to waste it.

Next, Whitney sang the first chorus. "Stick more to the basic melody for this one," I told her, and that's what she did. Then, for the second chorus, I suggested that she ad-lib something on the third line, and she did that, too. Afterward, we dealt with the first verse, for which we wanted to hear the details and the little melody changes that I had made. "Yeah, yeah, yeah. I've got it," Whitney said enthusiastically, almost breathlessly, when listening to the backing track, and after she sang that first verse three or four times and harmonized a line on the second verse, I exclaimed, "That's genius." Because it was. Listen to her rendition of "For the Love of You" and you'll hear a performance that's straight out of paradise—delivered within hours of her feeling physically and mentally drained. The transformation was miraculous.

The system that I employed to record Whitney's vocal on that song served as the template for virtually every number that we'd work on together, be it a romantic ballad or a kick-ass foot-stomper. What we'd usually end up with was a straight reading of the first verse, bridge, and chorus, so that we'd have the melody without embellishments. Then, for the second verse, bridge, and chorus, she would open up a little more before setting off those fireworks for the final chorus. It was like handling a thoroughbred racehorse— or a fine race car that at any moment might find that fifth gear, transporting us to a whole other level that would surprise even her. In effect, by coloring in all of the separate parts, we were painting a picture for the entire song.

Having been raised around Cissy, Dionne, and Aretha, Whitney knew what to do with a song as soon as she heard it, and like a porpoise in the ocean, she was really, really fast. When we collaborated, I tried to work quickly, too. The trick with Nippy was to capture her initial passion by not giving her enough time to really think about what she was doing, as well as to keep her excited about what she'd be doing next. I wanted her to have a good time because then we'd get that magic in the sound that would convince listeners she really *did* believe in what she was singing.

To Whitney's eternal credit, she always dedicated herself to giving me the very best. After making sure she stuck to the script when recording the separate parts, I would ask her to sing the song all the way through to see what more of her genius might come out. "Go beyond yourself," I'd encourage Nippy. "Try whatever you want and let's just see what we get." That's when the fifth gear often kicked in, producing a moment of sheer brilliance that I'd have to incorporate into the song. It was all about controlling and shaping the nature of her performance before racing down the home stretch.

As with all of the songs we worked on together, once Whitney had recorded her "For the Love of You" vocals, David Frazer and I stayed up all night choosing the best parts and compiling them so we had what sounded like a single take. It was rigorous work. The next morning, we listened to what we'd done and made some adjustments. When Whitney came in to hear the song, she was knocked out, remarking, "My God, it sounds finished!" She was right. "Yeah, all you've gotta do is this little riff and that little harmony, and you're done," I eagerly told her, purposely trying to pump her up and keep the momentum going.

Whitney and I had a really good chemistry for how to work fast together, and even if we had only a few hours on any given day, we could get most of a song—if not the whole song—done in that time. "I Wanna Dance with Somebody" was the next track she recorded. Whereas we'd established a mellow mood in the studio for her performance of "For the Love of You," this up-tempo, much more joyous number required us to grab Whitney's spirit when her soul was happy and excited. After playing the backing track and talking about what I wanted her to do for certain parts, we jumped straight in without allowing her to give it too much thought.

Again, letting Whitney's mind subdue her natural, spiritual passion would have been like pouring water on the fire. Instead, I wanted to capture as much as possible of that incredible spirit during the two or three hours when it peaked—usually in the middle of the day, between about four in the afternoon and seven in the evening—enabling her to go crazy, crazy, *crazy* on the vocals before then redoing specific parts that we wanted to take the time to think about. There had to be light and shade, which is why on the first verse, when Whitney sang, "Clock strikes upon the hour, and the sun begins to fade," she pulled back and used her little-girl voice. Then, when she got to the chorus, the strong woman appeared, her chest beating. The thing was, she actually sang the first verse *after* we'd captured—and pretty much exhausted—the raw power expended on the chorus, the bridge, and any other parts requiring that kind of voice.

These were the fireworks that I was hell-bent on getting in the bag before tackling the delicate stuff, and they included one of Whitney's fabulous improvisations for "I Wanna Dance with Somebody"—the "say you want to dance, don't you want to dance, say you want to dance" chant that earned her a vocal arrangement credit and resulted from just letting her go. It became the hook of the out chorus, and when Clive heard it, he loved how it took the song to an even higher level.

The fact was she was having fun, as you can tell by her laughing right near the end. That was Whitney's personality and her character. Once I knew she could do it so naturally, I asked her to laugh on other songs, too. I loved that sound. It was the sound of superhuman confidence in her own God-given talent; the sound of uninhibited appreciation for being divinely blessed; the sound of joy and liberation.

Following the session to record Whitney's lead vocal, we spent a short time the next day adding the finishing touches, including her backing vocals alongside those of Kitty Beethoven, Jim Gilstrap, Kevin Dorsey (who sang the bass part, "*dance*"), Myrna Matthews, and Jennifer Hall. I could see Whitney enjoyed watching them sing through the control room window, so I coaxed her to go into the main studio and join them.

When I listened to the finished track, it gave me goose bumps. "I Wanna Dance with Somebody" was full of Whitney's true sunshine energy, embellished with my energy as a drummer and that of the musicians around me. Just watch and listen to Randy Jackson on *American Idol* —"Yo, dog! That was *cool*, man!" I'm telling you, my whole crew had pick-me-up mojo, and it came through on the record.

"Just the Lonely Talking Again," an intimate ballad originally recorded by R&B vocal group the Manhattans, was very much a Clive Davis track. As he kept telling me, "I want a saloon singer in the spotlight at a tiny little club . . . Get Whitney to whisper." So, that's what I did, and once again, she made the song her own. Jazz composer Michael Gibbs arranged and conducted the background strings that subtly underpinned the main vocal, Kenny G contributed the understated tenor sax solo, and the result was sublime—smooth, sensual, sophisticated—with angel Whitney delivering precisely what Arista's main man had asked for.

As Clive would say, you always have to rein in the great singers because they have so much vocal capacity, and until they can hear what's going on and find the right approach, their natural instinct is to flex their chops. Whitney was no exception in that regard, needing to be reined in until she felt psychologically comfortable performing the whole number sweetly and softly—*whispering*—before letting loose near the end and hitting that fifth gear to provide the song with power while caressing it, too. In fact, she immersed herself so deeply in that track, all of her improvisations happened in one take. Not only was Whitney in the zone, she was beyond the zone. She entered a place where everything was so effortless and so perfect that anyone who heard it would say, "My God, this performance isn't humanly possible." She could channel the Divine.

Sitting with eyes closed, forefinger on lips, and listening intently while really wanting to believe in—and be touched by—what Whitney was singing, Clive looked like he had died and gone to Heaven when he first heard how she worked that sucker. Still, for Nippy one of the hardest things was to transition between songs, going from a turbo-powered track like "I Wanna Dance with Somebody" to putting on the lingerie, entering that seductive zone, and feeling as if she were barely singing on "Just the Lonely Talking Again." To help her relax, I'd give her one of those massages to which she was becoming increasingly accustomed while talking about whatever she wanted to discuss—God's presence in our daily lives, some of the new soul and R&B hits, you name it. Then, comfortable with the process and our brother-sister vibe, she'd invariably respond with the desired vocal performance. Mutual trust made for a heavenly friendship and unforgettable results.

After a lifetime in this business, I can honestly say that working up close and personal with an artist as talented as Whitney Houston was a rare privilege. Which is why the opportunity to also produce her duetting with Cissy on a cover of "I Know Him So Well" was something special. Written by Tim Rice together with Benny Andersson and Björn Ulvaeus of ABBA, this rousing ballad from the stage musical *Chess* had been a 1985 UK number one for

MARCH 1, 1987—"You're the most gift givingest man," Nippy would often tell me. Here, she cracks up over a teddy bear that would talk to her in my voice for twenty or thirty minutes, riffing on life in a very Southern ghetto drawl, while also asking her questions and making up his own answers.

DECEMBER 1986—Engineering maestro David Frazer watches me compile a track at Tarpan Studios as we listen to the best parts of what Whitney has just recorded for her self-titled second album.

JANUARY 1987—The best of friends, Whitney and Robyn Crawford enjoying some downtime in the back room at Right Track Recording in New York City during vocal sessions for the second album.

DECEMBER 1986—Taking a break at Tarpan Studios during the session to record the duet by Whitney and Cissy on "I Know Him So Well." While their love and respect for each other was self-evident, the constant joking and laughter made them appear more like sisters than mother and daughter.

FEBRUARY 24, 1987—Attending the 29th Grammy Awards with composer Burt Bacharach and Whitney's mom, Cissy. Burt won Song of the Year with Carole Bayer Sager for "That's What Friends Are For," and this was a really special get-together for Whitney and me because Burt and Cissy were among our main musical mentors, teachers, and sources of inspiration.

FEBRUARY 1987—"Here's how you do it." Jokingly helping Nippy to sign an autograph at Right Track, watched by bemused recording engineer Lincoln Clapp.

FEBRUARY 1987—Although Nippy and I liked to laugh and chat, the vast majority of our time in the studio was focused on the serious business of making music.

MARCH 1, 1987—Tracking the vocal for "So Emotional" at Right Track Recording in New York City. When I asked Nippy if she was nervous about how people would respond to her sophomore album, she calmly responded, "If they loved me the first time, they'll love me again."

1987—While our shared love of music resulted in divine smiles, Whitney's electrifying energy always lit up the room.

1988—Between the second and third albums, two kids still enjoying the whole parade of life.

MAY 1988—Backstage at London's Wembley Arena with Cissy and Prince Edward during Whitney's Moment of Truth World Tour. Moments earlier, I had made a guest appearance onstage, drumming to "I Wanna Dance with Somebody," but that didn't really interest Queen Elizabeth II's youngest child, who could hardly take his eyes off Princess Nippy.

Barbara Dickson and Elaine Paige, as well as the biggest-selling UK single ever by a female duo.

Despite Dickson assuming the role of the Russian chess champion's estranged wife, Svetlana, and Paige portraying his troubled mistress, Florence, the two women tracked their vocals separately and never actually met when recording the song. That, however, wasn't the case for the soul version featuring the Houstons. Having always loved the anthemic style of ballad—ranging from Little Anthony and the Imperials' "Goin' Out of My Head" to the Ronettes' "Be My Baby"—I was thrilled and appreciative of the chance to lay down a backing track onto which I could overdub timpani sounds, as well as strings arranged by the ingenious Mike Gibbs.

When it came to the vocals, standing in the studio area so they could see and sing to each other, Whitney and Cissy were clearly joyful to be sharing the spotlight. They had never duetted on a record before, but they had certainly done so many times onstage. What came through both audibly and visually—by way of the distinct sparkle in their eyes and how they occasionally, affectionately smiled at one another—was their mutual love and respect. It was as if they were being transported back to the days when they'd both sung in the church choir, to a time and place in their lives that had extra special meaning.

"It's the kind of feeling that you really can't explain," Cissy stated about their collaboration during a July 1988 NBC TV interview. "It goes so deep . . . It's just a magical kind of thing."

Whitney sang the first verse by herself; Cissy sang the second verse by herself. After performing a call-and-response on the first two choruses, they then duetted on the bridge and final chorus. Multiple takes enabled me to compile the best parts of their respective performances and showcase mother-and-daughter voices that, although contrasting significantly in terms of pitch and timbre—Cissy's being lower and somewhat smokier than Whitney's—blended wonderfully. Indeed, according to Nippy in the same NBC interview, when the tape was played back, "I couldn't tell who it was that was singing . . . I was like 'Oh, this is just too much for me.' It's very deep, you know. It's connected to the soul."

Whitney, who had inherited her musical genius from Cissy, was so happy and honored to work with her mom. And Cissy—a powerful woman who can be quite tough—felt equally privileged to be featured with her daughter on what would almost certainly be a hugely successful album. Instead of her role as the mother watching from the sidelines, she was now a part of everything and *killing it all the way*. Cissy was clearly very proud of Whitney, and it was fascinating to watch how she'd occasionally also draw on her greater experience to coach her: "Try it again and go a little higher if you want." The work was completed within a matter of hours, and the result was a perfect, majestic pop record, performed by two women whose frequent talking and laughter meant they often behaved more like sisters than mother and daughter.

After a week at Tarpan, Whitney returned home to the East Coast because she had some engagements there. Making things easy for her was always our bottom line. Having four tracks in the can was a great accomplishment, and our time together had been extremely positive, centering around a partnership between true music lovers who both did their level best to create the best record possible.

The following month, January 1987, would see us continue the job at Right Track in New York. There, we'd work on "Love Is a

Contact Sport," "Where Do Broken Hearts Go," and—although it wasn't yet on the schedule—"So Emotional." It promised to be another collaborative high and I, for one, could hardly wait.

"During this postmodern era, when the art of music has been replaced by the industry of entertainment, Whitney was one of those few people who was able to transform her artistic expression into a stream of musical intelligence. She was, probably, the technically best singer that I've been fortunate enough to work with. On '**Where Do Broken Hearts Go**,' I remember being awestruck hearing the difference between the basic track that we had worked on and the finished song featuring her vocals. Whitney was able to create those moments when music, musicians, singers, and listeners disappear, leaving only the awareness of being part of something that includes and transcends the individual. If it's true that it is not the object expressed but the depth of the subject expressing it that most defines art, then perhaps Whitney was the artistic representation of a unique and unrepeatable moment in music and time."

—CORRADO RUSTICI, guitarist

CHAPTER THREE

IF THEY LOVED ME
THE FIRST TIME

NE OF THE MAIN REASONS Whitney's initial visit to Tarpan Studios was so productive and successful, despite her post-tour fatigue, was the presence of Robyn Crawford. A tall, slim, beautiful woman with almond-shaped eyes, high cheekbones, and a radiant smile, Robyn had a deep love for Whitney and protected her from whatever and whomever she considered to be a negative force. She was the *true* bodyguard. She was also her soul sister, sharing a North Jersey apartment with Whitney, organizing her schedule, and generally being very supportive while ensuring Nippy showed up on time—or nearly on time—for all of her appointments. Having dropped out of Monmouth College—where she'd played basketball on a scholarship—to become her best friend's assistant (and eventually her creative director), Robyn covered a lot of bases for

Whitney in a really sweet, really sharp, really efficient, and really focused manner.

For me, another wonderful thing about Robyn was that, even though she enjoyed attending Whitney's recording sessions, she never got in the way. Most of my sessions are closed, and this was especially important with Whitney—I didn't want anyone or anything distracting her. Robyn, however, would sit on a couch at the back of the control room so that we couldn't see her. If asked for her opinion about a particular recording, she'd always have insightful things to say. Having her around therefore gave me confidence because I knew everything would be all right with Whitney.

Without exception, the only people in the studio when Whitney recorded her vocals were my engineer, Robyn, and myself. I didn't want Whitney to look at anybody else, try to please anybody else, or feel embarrassed by anybody else watching or listening to her. That's when ego enters the picture and the desired performance goes out the window. I wanted her to focus on what we needed, which became more of an issue when the sessions switched to Right Track in New York and Whitney's local family and friends could easily visit.

Among the people who'd drop by was her dad, John Russell Houston Jr., a showbiz exec from way back. He had managed the Sweet Inspirations, a vocal group Cissy founded, which sang backup to many great artists, including Elvis Presley, Aretha Franklin, Solomon Burke, Van Morrison, Wilson Pickett, Dusty Springfield, and Jimi Hendrix. It was John who, when Whitney was a toddler, had nicknamed her Nippy after a mischievous cartoon character. In 1986, he became her business manager and the CEO of her company, Nippy Inc.

Kind and soft-spoken, John was strikingly handsome as well as elegant and extremely dashing—a sophisticated, flawlessly beautiful blend of Cary Grant and Barack Obama. By the reverence Whitney would show him, I could tell he held all the cards and meant business. I'd stop the session whenever John showed up at the studio, giving father and daughter an hour or two to sit and talk.

The Whitney I witnessed in his presence was the little girl seeking guidance and protection within an industry that's always been known for the sharks circling its waters. "Are you taking care of yourself?" John would ask her. "Are you enjoying this whole thing? Is it going too fast for you?" He looked out for her, and she looked up to him. What's more, I could see elements of her in him, not least the charm, the confidence, and the super-smooth way of talking to people.

In future years, Whitney's parents' marriage would falter, and she and her dad would become estranged. At this time, though, all three of them still appeared to be very close. Certainly, John and Cissy were always really nice to me. "I'm just here to check on my daughter," one of them might say, at which point I'd tell everyone to take a break. Such visits didn't happen very often, however, because we all knew the music required 100 percent dedication to every note, every emotion. Fortunately, Whitney was in tune with my approach, and this included being patient about keeping the work to ourselves and not handing out cassettes of what we'd been recording until it had been completed to our satisfaction. Only then would we give Clive a copy.

In those days, Whitney didn't really have much input regarding the selection of material. Sometimes she'd like a song; sometimes she wouldn't. Once I'd coax her into singing something, though, she would be happy because suddenly she'd hear what she could do with it. At that point, we were home free. Still, getting her to put her voice on something could occasionally be very tricky.

"I don't really like this song so much."

"Okay, but you may feel differently once you've sung it."

"Nah, it's not my style."

"Then make it your style! C'mon, give it a try . . ."

Throughout the second album, aside from "For the Love of You," Whitney would come to the studio without really knowing the songs. Not overly convenient, but given how she was such a quick study, this was also not a problem. For each new number, I would break it down: "Sing the first verse." She would do this ten to twelve times to give me plenty of options to choose from. Then I'd say, "Sing the second . . . Sing the bridge . . . Okay, now blow me away for the ending!" Which is what she did, time after time.

In New York, at Right Track, Whitney consistently found that fifth gear. For example, I might have her perform five takes of a particular number in search of some extra dressing—"Okay, that was beautiful. Let's run through it again!" Well, the fourth or fifth one would frequently produce things that were miles ahead of whatever she'd given me before, even though those previous takes all had superb parts that would end up on the record. Consequently, despite the songs having already been recorded, there were times when I'd still build additional arrangements around Nippy's unplanned, improvised vocal fireworks, adding more horns, guitars, and backing vocals to match the new level that she'd established.

Whitney's divine side—her highest side, which was limitless— was so powerful during those moments of magic that it would shock the human in me, as well as the human in *her*. And it was so thrilling. I'd be like her cheerleader—leaping out of my chair, jumping up and down—doing whatever worked to encourage more of the same. She needed to feel raw emotion in return for what she was bringing to the number: "Goddamn, girl, that was *it*! Maybe we can now make those last few notes even better defined. Let's experiment . . ." At that point, it was about her singing things that had nothing to do with what we'd originally planned.

Listen to "Where Do Broken Hearts Go," a power ballad about trying to reignite a stalled romance, written by Frank Wildhorn—composer of the Broadway musical *Jekyll & Hyde*—and R&B singer Chuck Jackson. This song was one of the numbers that didn't meet with Whitney's approval when she first heard the demo. Quite simply, she didn't identify with the lovelorn lyrics and expressed her dissatisfaction to Clive during a meeting in his office. "I was saying, 'I don't want to sing this song. I don't like this song,'" she'd tell VH1 years later, "and he was going, 'But I'm telling you, this is going to be the song.' And it was. I went and recorded it, and to this day it is one of my favorite songs."

Whitney initially didn't like a lot of the songs that were selected for her to record. They were Clive's picks, and so it was usually a case of "How are we going to make this song work for *me*?" Not that we'd ever discuss it. I'd simply say, "I have a way of approaching the song that I think you'll like," and play her the track that I'd already recorded with another singer performing the guide vocal. Then Whitney could reinterpret it with greater soul and make the whole thing more believable.

That's what happened with "Where Do Broken Hearts Go." Reaching into the past as well as the present, I had chosen to give the track a spiritual yet contemporary sound. My goal was to convey purity, innocence, soulfulness, and warmth by indulging my love of bells and vibes to summon up the image of stained-glass windows, while making the outhouse come alive via synth keyboards, synth bass, synth guitar, and drum machines. Preston Glass—who assisted me throughout the project, playing some of the keyboards, programming the percussion, and arranging small string parts—helped me lay out all of the chords while also adding the bells and vibes. However, what Whitney then did with the song was incredible.

Aside from her ad-libs, all of the harmonizing and doubling of parts had been figured out beforehand when tracking the guide vocal back at Tarpan in California. Going into the session, I therefore knew what was required to make it sound like a real record, and Nippy was always happy to go along with that.

"Would you mind trying a double on this line?" I'd ask her.

"Sure."

"Let's do that again to make it a little tighter."

"Okay."

"This is a great line for the harmony."

"What harmony would you like?"

"Well, what do you hear?"

Whitney would suggest something, and I would say, "Great," happy that she'd provide the line with exactly what it needed. However, without having previously done my homework, I couldn't have been that sure-handed and that quick to make decisions. And thanks to the track having been recorded on the West Coast—where David Frazer captured the Cissy-like gospel backing vocals of Jim Gilstrap, Kitty Beethoven, Niki Haris, and

Jennifer Hall—we didn't have to waste time going, "What shall we do?" Instead, Whitney would be inspired by what she heard, and we'd work on stacking her vocals right away. Her ability to nail this was a gift numerous other artists don't have.

Even when she sang quietly, Nippy had the energy of a hummingbird. That's what gave her voice a fast, subtle vibrato—not the overt one that everyone could hear during the louder passages of a song, but one that the engineers and I didn't consciously notice in the studio until we'd rewind tape, replay her vocal in solo mode, and see a slight, rapid, constant trembling of the audio-level meter's needle. As with every number she performed, this delicate warbling instilled "Where Do Broken Hearts Go" with a resonance and vitality that I've never encountered in any other singer. Yes, Whitney had the range and the power, but this particular quality was one of the things that made her voice unique. Never mind that you couldn't really hear it—you could *feel* it.

Whereas Aretha had the rasp that the radio speakers loved, Whitney had this natural twitter on top of which she could also improvise a slow vibrato. Crafting a song that's simultaneously tender and powerful is a very delicate balance. The tender aspect is what makes it believable—"Where do broken hearts go, can they find their way home . . ."—while the power is what ensures it can be a contender for the Top Ten and even a number one. On this song, the bridge section is what sets up the finale: "And now that I am here with you I'll never let you go. I look into your eyes and now I know, *now I know* . . ."

The descending bass riff that counters Whitney's ascending voice on this line was inspired by my love of Motown and its legendary bass player James Jamerson, replicating the kind of part that he played on Marvin Gaye's "What's Going On." Then, immediately afterward, the vocal and instrumental pause when Nippy sings, "Where do broken . . . hearts go" is my touch. I'm a drummer and a rhythm freak, and those pauses create a sense of drama that captivates the listener. They're a space for God to talk. Following that pause toward the end of "Where Do Broken Hearts Go," you can hear how Whitney, now singing in a higher key, is caught in the fire, playing off the harmonies and sprinting for the finish line. From the sweet angel to the woman with balls—oh man, how she brought it home.

In the studio, I was her live audience, nodding my head and punching the air to communicate, "Everything is good. Go for it!" And she did. Whitney reached inside herself to extract the inspirational, and I'd feel excited for her. At the same time, giving her juice by showing the impact that her performance was having on *me*—being swept away by both the emotion and the raw power and giving her free rein to keep rolling with the feel—enabled us to connect through the control-room glass.

We worked hard together to get the right performance on "Where Do Broken Hearts Go," again recording it in sections, with the outro sung first to really open up her voice, hit that fifth gear, and capture the magic. She poured on everything she had. It took a couple of hours to be sure we had that gusto before assembling the rest of the puzzle for what we were hell-bent on making: a number one record.

Like Marvin Gaye, Stevie Wonder, and Michael Jackson, Whitney could shift almost effortlessly between her loud, powerful chest voice and her higher, lighter head voice. (Right Track engineer Lincoln Clapp used *EQ*—equalization—to appease my taste for bright-sounding vocals and to also ensure they weren't too shrill.) "Imagine you're making a movie and the camera's really close," I told Nippy when asking for those delicate parts where only the subtlest nuances were necessary. "The person you're singing to is right next to you, not across the room." Again, understanding precisely what I was saying, she delivered the goods, and the end result was otherworldly.

Next on the agenda was "Love Is a Contact Sport," an up-tempo R&B track with a self-explanatory title. "You gotta move in tight if you wanna do it right," the frustrated gal tells the slack guy she's been dating. Whitney was a woman who didn't mince her words—if she had something to say, she'd come straight to the point—and this number certainly echoed her voice. Preston Glass had written it specifically for her, and I knew its smokin' vibe and irresistible energy would be perfect for the album. What's more, I knew Nippy would transport it to another level.

When recording the song's backing track at Tarpan, I had tried to combine the fast-shuffle feel of a Martha and the Vandellas Motown number with a high-tech sound that used programmed drums, synth strings, and badass horns—all cutting-edge during the mid-'80s and, as evidenced on the record, perfectly suited to Whitney's youthful essence. She brought a lot of love to it, as did all of us who worked on the number, running through take after take, sometimes word by word, before we then had to decide which of the genius parts really were the cream of the crop. What you hear is an amalgam of the best of the best of the best. Choosing is confusing, but what a great problem to have with Whitney Houston. I would listen to each part only once during the editing process and go with my gut instinct, not allowing my mind to talk me out of anything.

By this time, with only one track left for us to work on, Whitney and I shared an increasingly close friendship. The conversation flowed freely in the studio whenever we took a break. And the air often filled with the sweet aroma of the crunchy orange chicken that she loved ordering from a local Chinese restaurant. Those were the occasions when she'd kick back and relax—confiding in Robyn, joking with me—while alternating between the streetwise gal who'd jump around the control room, impersonating Jellybean Benitez's moves on the dance floor, and the soft-spoken young princess of the ball, who'd squeal with delight at the teddy bears and other small gifts that I'd often give her. "You're the most gift givingest man," she would say while filling the air with her infectious laughter.

Still, we were dealing with really high stakes. We didn't fool around when it came to the music. We were on a mission. Once we had taken a quick break, we'd get back to the recording, with Whitney focused like a laser.

"What do you think about this section?" she might ask me while listening to a playback.

"I think we can do it again."

"What does it need?"

"You can maybe go a little higher."

"Fine, let's do it."

Fast-forward several minutes. "Now do you like what I've done?"

"I think it's genius!"

"Yeah, I like it, too."

We never talked about what Clive Davis or Arista or the rest of humanity might want. From "Hi" to "Bye," it was all about our love for the music and getting on with the job that *we* wanted to do.

When a vocal session was over, Whitney would stick around for maybe half an hour.

"Can you do push-ups?" I might ask her playfully.

"Hell, yeah."

"How many push-ups can you do?"

"How many do you want me to do?"

"Can you do twenty?"

"Hell, yeah."

Smirking cockily while giving me her playful, heavy-lidded look, she'd drop to the floor and do those push-ups without even pausing to take a breath.

While I felt comfortable and Nippy was so sweet, I was constantly mindful of making her feel safe. Like most of the artists I'd worked with, she had a fragile side, and I'd do whatever it took to alleviate the pressure and take care of her. This meant talking with her to help her feel comfortable as well as dealing with every aspect of a song, including the lengthy task of piecing together the one we'd been working on after Nippy said her good-byes and left for the day. There wasn't enough time to socialize or toast our next hit with a glass of red wine.

I'd stay at the studio until two or three in the morning sifting through the various takes, after which Lincoln Clapp would continue compiling and editing the puzzle until about six while I was asleep at my hotel. By nine, there'd be a tape waiting for me, and going over the notes I had previously written about which parts to use, I would stay in bed until eleven to listen to the vocal that Lincoln had assembled. Returning to the studio at noon, I'd do a rough mix of the vocal with the backing track and have this ready for Whitney's arrival at around four. Exhilarated by what she heard, she'd then feel energized to redo certain small parts and add the final touches.

It was an intense, round-the-clock schedule, at least for Lincoln and me. For Whitney, it was as easy as I could make it. Without a doubt, I wanted to keep working with her, so I tried to ensure that she enjoyed the work and would want to come back.

Our last assignment for the second album was "So Emotional," a high-tech, machine-dominated dance number that hadn't been part of Clive's original list, but which had been added between Whitney finishing her work at Tarpan and continuing it at Right Track. The song's composers, Billy Steinberg and Tom Kelly, had already enjoyed chart-topping successes with Madonna's "Like a Virgin" and Cyndi Lauper's "True Colors." In "So Emotional," Whitney obsesses about a dude with whom she's played hot and heavy. "Oh, I remember the way that we touch," she cries out. "I wish I didn't like it so much."

Bouncing back and forth between Stevie Wonder's growl—on lines such as "I like the *animal* way you move"—and her Michael Jackson–type rhythmic exclamations of "Uh" and "Ooh," Whitney really let it rip on this track. Here she was, drawing on some of her musical influences while showing off her own great sense of rhythm and singing at the very top of her range: "Ain't it shocking what *love can do?*" As always, what you hear on the record is Whitney's 100 percent artistic investment in what *she* was doing. She killed it. And I added her suggestive line at the beginning—"I don't know why I like it . . . I just do!"—for a touch of eroticism. Meanwhile, Walter Afanasieff's keyboards and Bongo Bob's percussion programming and drum sampling helped make that song more slammin', more intense for the dance floor, more *black*.

It was March 1, 1987, and Mick Jagger was working in an adjacent room at Right Track on his solo album *Primitive Cool*. At one point, having heard snatches of "So Emotional" bleeding through the studio walls—that's how loud we were cranking it out—he walked in during a playback, said a quick "Hi!" to Whitney, and then started jumping around to the track's infectious sound. At that time, it was ground-breaking to have so much power coming at you with a simultaneous blend of soul and funk rhythms and rock guitar. Mick recognized this, and unable to keep away, he danced all over the place like he was onstage. Nippy loved it. She cracked up at the sight of Mick doing his thing, and after she left I joined him again out in the lobby. "The song's fantastic," he remarked in that unmistakable London accent. I thanked him and nodded my agreement.

When first playing me the "So Emotional" demo, Clive had asserted, "If you produce this, it'll be a number one." Now, hearing the finished track in the studio, I was really excited that we had actually made it *sound* like a number one. Visiting Clive's Manhattan office—with its scenic views and prominently positioned wall photos of him with Miles Davis, Sly Stone, and Paul Simon—I therefore placed a cassette on the semicircular desk that was already piled with other cassettes.

Clive inserted the tape into one of his precisely calibrated TEAC machines. Eyes half-closed, forefinger on lip, he was immersed dreamily in the sound while I, standing and staring straight down at him, was finding it hard not to beat my chest in triumph. Silently, symbolically that's *precisely* what I was doing—here I was, delivering to the man who was my father, my older brother, my employer, exactly what he'd asked for: *a number one record*. Why the hell *shouldn't* I be proud?

It's not easy taking a track that, in demo form, is no chart-topper and transforming it into one after ensuring the artist will cooperate. You've got to jump through plenty of hoops to get from A to Z, and although I had a lot of respect for Clive, I just wanted to make sure he recognized the hard work that I'd put into fulfilling his vision so that he'd respect me, too. "You wanted it? You got it!" Talk about feeling the power like Muhammad Ali. Whitney, Clive, me—we were *all* champs.

When the song finished playing, Clive just looked up at me and said, "Congratulations, you've done a great job." This, I knew, was his typically understated way of giving praise, but judging by the satisfied smile on his face, I could tell he was thrilled with what he'd heard.

Not that this industry veteran was the only one to display a cool head amid the surrounding sense of achievement. During the sessions to record Whitney's "So Emotional" vocal, I'd asked her a potent question: "Are you in any way nervous about making this new album?" I mean, hell, the first record's success had been so huge, unlike anything I'd ever been a part of. Surely, I thought, this young woman must be feeling immense pressure—from the media, from the record company, from herself—to not only repeat her recent achievements but to also surpass them. Yet, she—*surprise!*—was totally self-assured. "No," she replied with characteristic nonchalance. "If they loved me the first time, they'll love me again."

This was the Whitney I knew and the Whitney I adored at the start of 1987—before her self-titled sophomore album was released, before her success and superstardom reached new heights

. . . and before some negative reaction from her own community hit her where it hurt, dented her innate self-confidence, and steered her in a different artistic direction.

"When we shot the video for '**So Emotional**,' everything from the rehearsals and choreography to the actual filming was a magical, unforgettable experience. In one scene, Whitney and I danced together, doing a move called 'The Snake' that was really popular back then, and when I heard her sing along to a playback of the song, I was amazed. She was so blessed with natural talent. In the studio, you'd just have to put a microphone in front of her and let the magic happen. At that time, there wasn't as much technology to fix one's playing or to tune and change the voice. We had to play and sing everything for real, and that's what makes the music of Whitney Houston so great and forever classic."

—TM STEVENS, bass guitarist

CHAPTER FOUR

MOMENT OF TRUTH

IPPY WAS STILL EARNING kudos for the first album, *Whitney Houston*, while we were finishing our work on her second, *Whitney*. She received five accolades at the American Music Awards show in Los Angeles on January 26, 1987, for Favorite Pop/Rock Female Artist, Favorite Soul/R&B Female Artist, Favorite Pop/Rock Album, Favorite Soul/R&B Album, and Favorite Soul/R&B Video. At the BPI Awards show in London on February 9, where she performed "How Will I Know," Whitney was voted Best International Solo Artist. And even though Steve Winwood's "Higher Love" beat her cover of "The Greatest Love of All" for Record of the Year at the Grammy Awards at L.A.'s Shrine Auditorium on February 24, her performance of the song received a standing ovation.

The success of Nippy's debut album had set a precedent: Coming off the back of three consecutive number one singles in the United States, she was serving as her own hard act to follow. For many artists, this would amount to unbearable pressure. How to live up to all the hype and expectations created by a stunningly successful debut record? How to avoid disappointing the fans? How to sustain musical credibility in the eyes of the critics? Whitney, of course, was no regular artist, either in terms of her talent or her attitude—she was confident in her ability and about the work she was doing, and man, did that ever prove to be *dead-on*!

When I first saw the colorful, exultant video for "I Wanna Dance with Somebody" on the Tarpan control room's big screen, I thought Nippy looked so beautiful with her curly, curly hair, and so delightfully happy. Thanks to the directorial efforts of my friend Brian Grant—who had also helmed the video for Aretha's "Freeway of Love"—Whitney virtually jumped off the screen.

I'd never seen other artists suffer the wear and tear that she sustained from all of the touring, recording, and publicity interviews. But then they weren't Whitney Houston at that time, when everybody—including me—wanted a piece of her. In the video, I could see that she was back to being her real self—the vibrant, fun-loving person I knew—and the sound coming through Tarpan's large speakers was totally great, capturing what we had done in the studio. "This," I thought, "is going to be *massive*." And it was.

Released on April 30, 1987, as the leadoff single to help promote the *Whitney* album that would be in stores on June 2, "I Wanna Dance with Somebody" commenced a two-week stay atop the Billboard Hot 100 on June 27, the same day that Nippy became the first female artist to have an album debut at number one on the Billboard 200, where it remained for the next eleven weeks. These twin successes were really powerful in both of our lives—confirming the fact that she was picking up where she'd left off with her previous album and helping to cement my own growing reputation as a hit producer. *Whitney* also debuted at number one in the UK and topped the charts in ten other countries around the world. "I Wanna Dance with Somebody" managed the same feat in eleven countries worldwide. Quickly becoming one of Nippy's signature songs, it was her biggest-selling single up to that time and, to this day, trails only "I Will Always Love You" in that category.

My production of "For the Love of You," a cover of the Isley Brothers' 1975 record, was originally slated to be the next single. Instead, Arista decided to capitalize on Whitney's success with original material and released the power ballad "Didn't We Almost Have It All," by Michael Masser and Will Jennings, on August 13. By the end of the following month it, too, topped the Billboard Hot 100.

Now Clive and his A&R colleagues knew they could really pour it on. That November, "So Emotional" was issued as a single, promoted by a video directed by Wayne Isham, who had helmed videos by Mötley Crüe, Bon Jovi, and Judas Priest. It showed Nippy supposedly preparing for a concert and performing at Lehigh University's Stabler Arena in Bethlehem, Pennsylvania, before 2,500 rabid fans. A three-tier stage was constructed after seventeen days of summer rehearsals had taken place at the arena in preparation for the October 20 and 21 filming. The band included the great Vernon "Ice" Black on rocking lead guitar, the mighty TM Stevens on bass, my brother Gigi Gonaway on percussion, and me on drums.

I had worked with Isham before, and it was great to be reunited with him. It was also a delight to be appearing in my first video with Whitney, giving us the chance to laugh and clown around on the set and in the dressing room. On the first day of filming, we shot the rehearsal scenes in our casual clothes. There was no audience, so all of us could work on bits of business for the live performance, such as Whitney leaning on Ice while he was playing and executing some dance moves with him and TM. When the fans came in the next day, we were in high-performance mode, and I loved seeing the audience explode in response to Whitney's presence and the ultraloud playback of the "So Emotional" recording. Wow, what a sound! I was sure that it would be a smash and the same went for Nippy. She was in rare form—as vibrant and bubbly as you see her in the video.

Played in heavy rotation on MTV and VH1—during a pre-Internet/YouTube era when television was the only means of viewing such material—the visibility and popularity of the video certainly contributed to "So Emotional" becoming the first U.S. number one of 1988. This placed Whitney in a three-way tie with the Beatles and the Bee Gees for the record of six consecutive U.S. chart-toppers, which she then smashed on my birthday, April 23, when "Where Do Broken Hearts Go" reached pole position on the Billboard Hot 100. At that point, Nippy was the only artist in history to have seven successive U.S. number ones, as well as the first female to have four of them released off the same album (with three produced by yours truly).

Witnessing all of this happen, I was floored. Sure, I knew we were dealing with a red-hot album, and, yes, I was proud that I had helped deliver some chart-topping singles. However, even though I had produced the most successful record of Aretha's career, the million-selling *Who's Zoomin' Who?*, I'd never seen or been around anything quite like this. With her sophomore effort, Whitney became one of the top female stars of the 1980s, surpassing the likes of even Madonna by enjoying a combined twenty-five weeks on top of the Billboard 200 with her first two albums.

At the Grammy Awards, staged inside New York's Radio City Music Hall on March 2, 1988, Whitney won Best Female Pop Vocal Performance for "I Wanna Dance with Somebody," and I was named Producer of the Year (Nonclassical). This was in recognition of my work not only with Nippy, but also on Aretha's self-titled album—which won her the award for Best Female R&B Vocal Performance—and her duet with George Michael "I Knew You Were Waiting (For Me)." Judged to be Best R&B Performance by a Duo or Group with Vocal, this transatlantic chart-topper had replaced another one of my productions atop the Billboard Hot 100—Starship's "Nothing's Gonna Stop Us Now." I was on a roll.

Imagine Quincy Jones and Michael Jackson sitting together in the front row when my name was announced over theirs (for Michael's *Bad* album) and those of the other nominees. I was in shock. Initially rooted to my seat, I managed to get up while "I Wanna Dance with Somebody" blasted over the P.A. and an ecstatic Whitney kept calling my name. *I need to get up on that stage*, I remember thinking as she hugged and kissed me. Quincy then wrapped his arms around me as I neared my destination. Peering over his shoulder, I could see Michael smiling graciously. What a moment. This was the pinnacle of my career, and I was *elated*. Finally making it onto the stage, I accepted my precious Grammy and launched into a hastily improvised speech.

"How you like me *now*?" I jokingly asked the audience before dedicating the award to my maternal grandmother, Nellie, as well as to my spiritual inspiration, Sri Chinmoy. Time was limited, and my mind was racing. Deciding to keep it simple, I wrapped things up by thanking my managers, David Rubinson and Greg DiGiovine; my wife, Anukampa; and "all the great artists who've helped me, all the great producers along the way . . ."

Backstage, everyone was suddenly interested in talking to me, including the likes of Quincy, Michael, and Sinéad O'Connor. *Rock royalty.* It was as if the doors to a members-only club had been unlocked and I now belonged on the inside. At the same time, a couple of people also warned me that I may have screwed up by not specifically thanking Clive Davis for the role that he'd played in my success. It's quite possible that Clive *was* upset about not being mentioned, but I also didn't mention Whitney, Aretha, George Michael, Starship, or anyone else with whom I'd worked. If I offended Clive, I wish to apologize. But, feeling nervous and rushed, I quite simply finished my speech as fast as I could.

By now, Whitney had completed the North American leg of her Moment of Truth World Tour, named after a midtempo number that fired her up—"This is our moment of truth. Either we win or we lose this love . . ."—but which had been relegated to the B-side of the "I Wanna Dance with Somebody" single. Written by Jan Buckingham and David Paul Bryant, this positive affirmation of love was set to a cool groove that I'd produced at Tarpan, and Whitney had really enjoyed recording it. When the song didn't make the cut for the album, I wasn't surprised that she used its title for the tour.

This kicked off in Tampa, Florida, on July 4, 1987, traveling to arenas, amphitheaters, coliseums, and convention centers all over the United States and Canada through the first week of December. As on her first world tour, Nippy performed on a circular stage in the center of each venue, this time backed by a seven-piece band

and accompanied by three dancers. After a four-month break, the tour then resumed in Europe on April 17, 1988, commencing with Belgium before moving on to the Netherlands and the UK, where her schedule included nine nights at London's Wembley Arena starting on May 4.

I happened to be in London at the same time as Nippy for a *Top of the Pops* BBC TV appearance to promote my own UK Top Ten hit, "Divine Emotions." Beforehand, I spent a couple of days rehearsing my moves with a trio of dancers at the AIR Studios complex of Beatles producer George Martin, where I had once recorded with both Jeff Beck and the Mahavishnu Orchestra. Having already begun work at Tarpan on a song titled "One Moment in Time"—which Whitney had been commissioned to record as a theme for the U.S. Olympic and Paralympic teams competing that summer in Seoul, South Korea—I therefore called her and suggested we should track her vocal at AIR. As Mike Gibbs was also in town, we'd even be able to have him arrange and conduct the London Symphony Orchestra there. "This'll be a blast," I told Nippy. She agreed. During the same phone conversation, sounding as if she'd been energized by her concert audiences—"They're just so loving, so passionate."—she asked me to come see her show, which is what I did that very night.

Backstage at Wembley Arena, I was invited to join Whitney and her band for the encore to play "I Wanna Dance with Somebody." This would be the first time I'd drummed for her in a full concert setting—no way could I decline the offer. However, I was so pumped up with nervous anticipation that, when it came to the actual performance, I pounded the crap out of the drums and nearly broke the kit. For me—and for the kit—it was an unforgettable experience, enhanced by a postshow get-together with Cissy and Queen Elizabeth II's youngest child, Prince Edward. The prince was so goggle-eyed over Princess Nippy, he looked as if he'd like to relinquish his royal duties and escape to a desert island with her.

That, of course, was impossible—she had a date at AIR to record "One Moment in Time." Written by the veteran team of Albert Hammond and John Bettis, this regal anthem saluted self-belief, unbridled ambition, dogged determination, and whatever else is required to defy the odds and "seize that one moment in time. Make it *shine*." For inspiration, Hammond had imagined Elvis Presley performing the song in lavish style at the Olympics' opening ceremony. Now, as the lead track on the *1988 Summer Olympics Album: One Moment in Time*—featuring contributions by, among others, the Four Tops, the Bee Gees, Jennifer Holliday, Jermaine Jackson, and Kashif Saleem—the song would provide the perfect opportunity for Whitney to dig deep and give the kind of inspirational performance that only a select few can deliver.

Since the record was scheduled for an August release, Clive wanted to hear the recording as soon as possible—a recording for which I had recruited more than a dozen musicians and singers to record the backing track at Tarpan. It was a huge production, and one that was about to become even larger with the addition of majestic brass and strings, engineered at AIR by Jon Jacobs.

Before we began working there, I decided to help Nippy relax by playing her my "Divine Emotions" promo video that featured me dancing and driving along a stretch of Californian coastline. It worked. She loved it, giggling and squealing at the sight of my well-choreographed moves. This put her in the perfect mood to go over "One Moment in Time" section by section. Because she'd already familiarized herself with the song's demo, there wasn't much for her to learn. Yet, despite our prior studio experiences, I was still astonished by how effortlessly and beautifully she handled the long notes toward the end, especially given the regular strain being placed on her voice by the ongoing live shows. It was incredible: She sounded as magnificent as ever.

The session caught Whitney at the very height of her powers. At one point, George Martin dropped by and was amazed by her vocal prowess, infusing a pop ballad with the gospel that she had been steeped in all of her life. "To taste the sweet I face the pain," she sang with contradictory ease before laying down, "I will feel eternity." This, truly, was history in the making.

That same day, we tracked the orchestral overdubs, featuring high piccolo trumpets, inspired by David Mason's resplendent solo on the Beatles' "Penny Lane," to complement the timpani and chimes that had been recorded at Tarpan. I wanted "One Moment in Time" to be the biggest, baddest, most over-the-top theme in Olympic history, and that's what Whitney and I heard when we listened to the mix that incorporated all of the various elements. Nippy, the rhythm section, the backing singers, and the orchestra were just killing it.

With the track in the can, Whitney departed from the UK in mid-May to perform tour dates in France, Germany, Denmark (where Crown Prince Frederik obtained special leave from his military academy to attend her show), Norway, Sweden, and Italy. Then, on June 11, amid concerts in Rome and Milan, she flew back to London to wow 72,000 people with a stunning performance at Wembley Stadium for the all-star 70th Birthday Tribute to the still-imprisoned South African anti-apartheid activist Nelson Mandela.

The European leg of the tour ended with shows in Austria, Switzerland, Germany, and Spain through June 29, when an exhausted Nippy finally returned to the United States and recharged her batteries at her home in Mendham, New Jersey. Only then did I tell her during a phone call that, after I had delivered the recording of "One Moment in Time" to Clive back in late-May, he'd told me he wanted her to redo the first verse so that it adhered more to the basic melody.

"*What?*" she cried. "You and I both agreed that vocal is perfect!"

It was true, but what could I do?

"Clive knows what he wants, and he makes the final decision," was all I could say.

"I don't believe this," Whitney muttered in an exasperated voice. "Okay, whatever." She sounded too tired to argue.

I visited her at home that July to rerecord part of the "One Moment in Time" vocal in her small, brand-new basement studio. The house that Nippy had purchased the previous year didn't look overly large when I stood in front of it. However, after an assistant greeted me at the door and I was inside that sucker, I could see it stretched on and on and on—12,500 square feet situated on five acres of land, with stained glass in the entrance lobby that adjoined the high, circular rooms with floor-to-ceiling windows. These included an enormous kitchen, five bedrooms, and five bathrooms in addition to a swimming pool, hot tub, four-car garage, and parking for more of her fleet of barely-driven motor vehicles: a Jaguar, a Mercedes, you name it. It looked like an auto showroom, and I was awestruck by how fast she'd acquired all of this.

The studio, little more than a vocal booth, was off a really, really long corridor where the walls were fit from top to bottom, end to end, with cabinets to accommodate the awards that Nippy had received from around the world. To say it was an impressive sight would be a colossal understatement. Only a handful of the most celebrated artists could compete with what this young megastar had accomplished during the past few years. So, you can imagine how intimidated I felt standing there with my East Coast engineer, Lincoln Clapp, and Whitney, who was making it perfectly clear she still wasn't convinced about redoing the vocal on which she had already worked so diligently.

"It doesn't make any sense," she complained, her voice barely concealing how pissed off she felt about having to give up her free time to satisfy the Arista boss's wishes. "Nothing's wrong with it."

"Okay, but it's important to Clive," I reiterated as delicately as possible.

"I don't care. He knows I'm worn out."

"Look, my love, if you'll just be open to singing the first verse three times with the straight melody, I'm sure I can insert the parts I need to please him and make everybody happy. It honestly won't take long."

"I don't wanna do it, and I don't *have* to do it."

"I hear you, but Clive's convinced we can make this incredible record even stronger, and we want him to be happy so he does everything to promote it. Three takes is all we'll need to bring out the melody he wants to hear, and it'll be worth it because then he'll feel like he's a part of it."

"Aw, damn . . . All right."

"Thank you, thank you. I'll make it as painless as possible."

While I was saying this, I was actually massaging Nippy's hands. You couldn't force her to do something. You could ask her if she'd cooperate and, if you were nice about it, she *would* cooperate. However, you'd have to treat her with kid gloves because, like so many supergifted people, she was very sensitive. Muhammad Ali's legendary trainer Angelo Dundee couldn't say, "Champ, I want you to do more jabbing." He'd say, "Champ, your jab looks *great* today."

"It does look great, doesn't it?"

"Yeah, it sure does."

That's how he'd get him to jab more, and it was the same with Whitney. You'd have to flip her around. I didn't want her to think, "Who the hell are *you*?" She could choose at any time to work with somebody else. I was, therefore, always very humble in her presence, and this apparently had the desired effect when, for the first and only time, I was forced to contend with her defiant insistence that she would *not* do something I'd asked her to do.

As soon as he saw Nippy enter the vocal booth, Lincoln set up an AKG C12 microphone like the one she'd used at AIR and ensured the sound matched what she had recorded there. Then, after she'd reacquainted herself with the song—going over the words, humming the melody—we did a take of her running through the first verse. "Excellent," I said. "Okay, now try focusing more on the straight melody." That's what she did. "Perfect," I commented. "Now, one more time, making it breathy and very, very tender." Again, she had no problem giving me what I'd asked for. "That's great, my love," I told her. "You're done. When I've inserted some of the parts you've just recorded it'll sound like an all-new verse. Thank you *so much*."

Whitney returned upstairs, and along with Lincoln, I began editing and compiling in her basement studio—running through what she'd just recorded, selecting the best parts, and using them to reassemble the song's first verse. About an hour in, I received a call from a household assistant asking if we wanted some food to be brought down. "No, thanks," I replied. "When we're finished in an hour, hour and a half, that'll be the time to take a quick break."

"Fine, not a problem," the assistant said.

Sure enough, about an hour and a half later, we finished compiling the track, and I called the assistant to say we were now ready to have whatever food and drink she wanted to bring downstairs. The person who appeared next, however, was Whitney, and she wasn't carrying a tray. She had a stone-cold look on her face, and the heavy-lidded gaze that accompanied her motioning for me to join her in the corridor—the corridor with all of her achievements staring me straight in the face—told me something was bugging her big time. *Whoo! Steam, baby, steam!*

"This is *my* home," she growled, while the hairs stood up on the back of my neck.

"I know this is your home," I answered calmly, almost inquisitively, never having seen her dark side directed at me this way.

"This is where I *live*."

"I know, honey. What's the problem? The work's done, you did great, everything's worked out just fine."

"You're in *my* home."

"If it's about the food, we couldn't eat it because we were right in the middle of our work."

"Look, I didn't appreciate doing any of this in the first place! How *dare* people just come here and do whatever they want!"

"I'm sorry, I didn't realize . . ."

"I don't want you thinking you can come in here and tell me what to do in my own home!"

"I know. I know. And *you* know I love and respect you. If what I've done has upset you or anyone else, that wasn't my intention."

"Okay, but this is my home. This is *my home!* This is *my house!*"

"I'm sorry. I promise, whatever it is that's upset you will never happen again . . ."

That's for sure, she must have been thinking while staring me down.

Whoa! Was all of this really due to some *damned sandwiches?* Despite trying my best to calm Nippy down, nothing I said appeared to work. I must have said I was sorry about thirty times while she just kept blowing off steam. Burned out from the tour, she'd done what had been asked of her while resenting how Clive had reached invisibly into her private sanctuary, during her hard-earned relaxation time, to force her to correct something she didn't think needed correcting. Deep down I think she knew he was just doing his job, and the same went for me, but she was sick and tired of being told what to do, and having this happen in her own home had pushed her over the edge.

As a touring musician, I myself knew what it's like to be on planes, trains, and buses while people make their demands every minute of the day and night. It's exasperating, and Whitney had reached the point where she was totally done with the whole thing. Nevertheless, having been hired by Clive to take care of an A-list project, I also had to trust in his proven musical judgment and deliver what he wanted.

The revised version of "One Moment in Time" confirmed that had now been achieved, with me paying the price for appearing to be more on Clive's side than on Whitney's. I'd been trying to please the two of them, but in this case it just wasn't possible. Therefore, after I once again reassured her that we had accomplished everything we'd set out to do and thanked her for her time, love, and effort, Lincoln and I collected our belongings and left. That was the only occasion during all the years I knew Whitney that I ever saw her rage on and on and on about anything. She was so mad, so upset, she just couldn't find the off switch.

Toward the end of August, "One Moment in Time" was released as a single, and the song eventually went Top Five in the U.S. while becoming Nippy's third number one in the UK. Despite her unhappiness when finishing that record, it was as if she could do no wrong. Meanwhile, on August 28, she performed a Madison Square Garden benefit concert that raised a quarter of a million dollars for the United Negro College Fund, aiding both African-American students and historically black universities. This wasn't the first time she'd assisted the UNCF—the photographer who'd helped launch her modeling career spotted her during an early-1980s charity concert for the same organization at Carnegie Hall.

Now, however, there were increased rumblings within the black community that Whitney's crossover success was being achieved at the expense of her ethnic identity. According to some, her music "lacked soul," while others put things more succinctly by asserting she was "too white." What bullshit. To me, this was jealousy plain and simple on the part of some small-minded knuckleheads who should have been proud of the world's most beloved singer.

"What do they want me to do?" Whitney asked during a July 1988 NBC TV interview. "I think music is music. I mean, how do I sing more black? Or what am I doing that makes me sound white? I don't understand. I'm singing music from my heart, from my soul, and that's it. So, I don't really think it's an issue in my life."

It shouldn't have been. But unfortunately, that's what it soon became. After completing her Moment of Truth World Tour with concerts in Japan, Australia, and Hong Kong through the end of November, Whitney was greeted enthusiastically when performing "Hold Up the Light" with BeBe and CeCe Winans during the NAACP Image Awards show at L.A.'s Wiltern Theatre on December 10. Then, on February 22, 1989, with her *stunning* rendition of "One Moment in Time," she brought the Grammy audience to its feet at the Shrine Auditorium. However, only seven weeks later at that same location, the vibe was totally different when Nippy attended the 3rd Annual Soul Train Music Awards. She met her future husband, Bobby Brown, at that event, but if love was in the air, it certainly wasn't coming from the predominantly black audience.

When Whitney's name was announced in conjunction with "Where Do Broken Hearts Go" being nominated for Best R&B/ Urban Contemporary Single, Female, numerous fools actually booed while a clip of the song's video was played. They needn't have worried—Anita Baker's "Giving You the Best That I Got" won the category. But that didn't alter the fact that catcalling Whitney was a lousy, mean-spirited reaction to someone who had never turned her back on her own people, let alone crossed into musical territory that hadn't already been mined by the all-powerful King of Pop, Michael Jackson.

The negativity hit Whitney hard—so hard that I soon heard through the Arista grapevine about her demanding to meet Clive Davis and fellow Arista executive Donny Inner to discuss it. Their response: Because she was a huge star, adored around the world, there was no need to panic or blow things out of proportion.

They were right. Black radio, pop radio—everyone loved Whitney Houston. However, hip-hop and a more hard-core strain of R&B were now becoming part of the mainstream, and their practitioners helped define the kind of screw-you attitude that surfaced at that Soul Train show: "You ain't hip-hop, you ain't rappin', you ain't got gold teeth, you ain't really ghetto." That's the attitude that stopped Whitney in her tracks and made her reassess her position: *Wait a minute, am I addressing my ghetto people?* The fact is, as a no-nonsense, speak-her-own-mind street girl, she really did want to be down with the ghetto cats as much as she enjoyed being on the Onassis boat.

What she'd been recording up until now was mainly pop material that Clive had picked and producers such as myself had then "ghettofied" by making the tracks sound nasty. A hybrid, a compromise—call it what you like; it clearly appealed to a mass market at home and overseas. Yet suddenly Whitney was being made to feel as if she'd been selling out. Although nothing could have been further from the truth, once the seed had been planted inside her brain it took root, and with her pushing to go more hard-core, it took root inside Clive's brain, too. It was hard to say no to Whitney.

She never said anything to me about this, and we never discussed it. For her next album, though, I'd find myself being asked to not only give a particular song the soul/bluesy Anita Baker kind of treatment but also to cut it four different ways in a desperate attempt to find the right vibe. Quincy Jones had once taught me, "You can't argue with a number one. Anything that's a number one, you've got to put your personal tastes aside, because enough people out there are responding to it for you to become a student and learn from that success." Now, however, we were about to mess with the success formula. And while I had bought into the whole "If they loved me the first time, they'll love me again" sensibility, the writing was on the wall and things would never be quite the same.

"For 'All the Man That I Need,' we sang the backing to Whitney's finished vocal, and capturing the right feel was not only down to our ability but also Narada's production skills, ensuring the call-and-response between us sounded authentic. Singing on her records and being privy to her vocals long before the general public got a chance to hear them was a real privilege. During those early years, I just loved the purity of Whitney's voice as well as her ability to take a simple line and make it sound really emotional. That's truly a gift. She was one of those singers who could perform 'Three Blind Mice,' and by the time she was finished, you'd be going, 'Wow, I've never heard it sound like *that* before!' It's one thing to impress people with a whole bunch of vocal riffs and vocal licks—that's what a lot of today's young singers do, and it's just a matter of learning the right mechanics. But to be able to take a simple melody, sing it straight, and in that moment make everybody feel the emotions are real is a special skill and a serious talent."

—CLAYTOVEN RICHARDSON, vocalist

CHAPTER FIVE

GOT SO MUCH SOUL

HILE WHITNEY CONTINUED TO feel the heat from certain half-witted sections of the black community for sounding "too white" on her records, her massive success had another downside: The music she was making generated widespread admiration within the industry, but it also intimidated some of her peers.

On May 1, 1989, a little over two years after I'd enjoyed the privilege of producing Whitney singing with her mom on "I Know Him So Well," I felt totally psyched about an opportunity to capture her duetting with her "Aunty Ree-Ree," the Queen of Soul, Miss Aretha Franklin. Involved in various other projects while Nippy had been completing the Far East leg of her Moment of Truth World Tour, I hadn't had much contact with her recently, and this would be a nice way for us to reconnect while doing something we certainly hadn't done before.

The location was the United Sound studio in Aretha's hometown of Detroit, Michigan, where I was co-producing some of the songs for her album *Through the Storm*. These included "Gimme Your Love"—which I wrote with Jeffrey Cohen and featured her singing alongside the Godfather of Soul, Mr. James Brown—and the title track, a duet with Elton John, written by Albert Hammond (co-composer of "One Moment in Time") and Diane Warren. This same team, which had penned Starship's "Nothing's Gonna Stop Us Now," was responsible for the Aretha/Whitney R&B stomper "It Isn't, It Wasn't, It Ain't Never Gonna Be."

At the time, my wife, Anukampa, and I owned a health food store, and I brought a basket full of goodies, which I gave to Whitney when she and Robyn arrived at United Sound. Nippy was so happy: "You're the most gift givingest man," she purred while dipping into a selection of organic bath and body products.

When Aretha arrived in her fur coat, cigarette holder in hand, I was at the mixing console, and Whitney was relaxing, sitting cross-legged on the control room floor.

"Oh, *hi* Queen!" I said enthusiastically.

"Where is she?" came the deadpan reply as she looked me square in the eye.

"You mean Whitney? She's right *here*."

Here was next to me, close to where Aretha was standing. Slowly redirecting her gaze from me to her honorary niece, she then said, "So, *you're* Miss Houston."

"Aunty Ree!" Nippy cooed like a little girl.

"Mm-hmm," Aretha nodded slowly with a smoldering look in her eyes. "Mm-hmm."

This all happened very quickly, but it was like a prizefighter staring down an opponent and saying, "You're messin' with me in my domain, and I don't appreciate it." I could tell Whitney didn't appreciate it, either. The quick glance that she shot me when Aretha looked the other away silently intimated, "What the hell's *her* problem?"

Clive had come up with the idea to have Aretha and Whitney duet on a song that would portray these two women fighting over the same man, which was kind of ridiculous given the age difference. However, while Nippy had agreed to do this and was in Aretha's neck of the woods out of genuine love—"This is my *family*"—the competition between divas runs *deep*.

We rolled tape, and the two women did their thing in front of the mics, taking turns singing, duetting, and interacting with one another as if they were buddies from way back. Several takes were recorded. Then on the last one, toward the end of the song—immediately after the Queen did some jazz-style scatting and Whitney interjected with "That's Aretha"—Nippy vamped a staggering vocal lick that would be hard to match, let alone outdo.

Without a doubt, she was still upset by how she had been treated, and this was evident when, as soon as her work had been completed, Whitney gave me a hug, said a quick good-bye to her aunt, and departed the session early. I felt a little awkward, but without pausing to take a breath, Aretha turned to me and said, "Go to the part of the tape where she did that thing and punch me in right after it."

So, that's what we did. Aretha reared back and performed an absolutely phenomenal riff before saying, "Do it again!" She didn't normally work like this, but we ended up doing eight takes right on that spot to make sure that, where Whitney had just knocked her—and everyone else—out, Aretha had a comeback: *Bring it on!*

Shortly after leaving the studio, Aretha called me on the phone while I was assembling the track, another thing that she'd never normally do.

"Was I too hard on her?"

"Yes."

"You think I should call her?"

"Yes."

Aretha felt bad, and I subsequently heard from Robyn that she had indeed called Whitney. I respected her for that. All of us were in awe of Aretha's talent, including Nippy, who in no way wanted to beat up on her aunt, but the Queen's competitiveness had gotten the better of her.

For her part, Whitney was becoming more hardened to the realities of life as the reigning number one pop diva. The black backlash against her music caused her to be increasingly frustrated with having her artistic motivations and personal beliefs misinterpreted. Consequently, a change was gonna come, even though I had no way of knowing this.

Sometime around June 1989, a large envelope arrived in the mail containing a poster-sized invitation with Nippy's photo:

> You are cordially invited to attend an outdoor barbeque
> in celebration of Whitney Houston's twenty-sixth birthday,
> Saturday, August 12, from 4 p.m. Dinner served at 8:30 p.m.
> Dress summer vogue. Tennis and swimming available.
> This invitation is nontransferable.

MAY 1, 1989—All smiles for the camera after Nippy finished recording the vocal for her duet with Aretha Franklin (Aunty Ree) on "It Isn't, It Wasn't, It Ain't Never Gonna Be."

MAY 1, 1989—At Detroit's United Sound before the Queen of Soul, Aretha Franklin, arrived to record a duet with her honorary niece. At the time, I owned a health food store with my wife, Anukampa, and she put together a basket for Nippy containing plenty of goodies.

AUGUST 12, 1989—My brother Kevin (right) watches as I hug Nippy at her twenty-sixth birthday party . . . three days after her actual birthday. The guests included both Eddie Murphy and Bobby Brown.

1990—My then-wife Anukampa Lisa Walden and Whitney enjoying a "pizza break" during sessions for "All the Man That I Need" at Right Track. They became such good friends, Guru Sri Chinmoy called them spiritual sisters.

1990—During the Right Track sessions for "All the Man That I Need." When I showed Whitney a copy of this photo, she immediately inscribed it: "Narada makes his sexy face."

1990—Laying down a vocal at Right Track Recording.

1990—When recording the vocals for her third album, *I'm Your Baby Tonight*, Whitney was still at the peak of her powers. And we were both still so happy to have yet another opportunity to work together.

OCTOBER 23, 1990—Attending the listening party celebrating *I'm Your Baby Tonight* at the Beverly Hills Hotel, in the company of (from left to right) Stevie Wonder, Babyface, Whitney, L.A. Reid, and Clive Davis. The genuine smiles mirror my pride in our collective achievements on Whitney's third album.

FEBRUARY 24, 1998—Attending Clive Davis's pre-Grammy Awards party with Tony Bennett and Bobby Brown. Tony, who frequently commented that Whitney was one of his favorite singers, told me he was completely floored by her talent. I guess we all were.

EARLY 2000s—Our friendship always endured, and we never had any lows, only highs. That's Bobby checking us out.

EARLY 1990s—I'm very proud of this shot, which Whitney inscribed, "My Sweet Narada, May God always smile on you & yours. Love always, Whitney."

August 12, 1989, was a Saturday, which is why the party took place at Nippy's New Jersey home three days after her actual birthday. This was inside a white canopy tent at the rear of the property that was so huge it looked like the circus was in town. Anukampa, my brother Kevin, and I were there along with about five hundred guests, including Natalie Cole, Jellybean Benitez, Ashford and Simpson, BeBe and CeCe Winans, Robyn Crawford, Dionne Warwick, and all of Whitney's close relatives.

When "I Wanna Dance with Somebody" kicked off the proceedings, the whole place exploded and I was really thrilled—any record that's a global smash obviously has a major impact, but seeing it up close like that was still totally amazing. Meanwhile, just as excited was the hostess, dressed in a form-fitting white outfit, and dancing to the record with none other than R&B singer-songwriter Bobby Brown, whom she had met earlier in the year at that infamous Soul Train Awards show.

This was one of the first times Nippy had seen Bobby since then, and she certainly looked happy that he'd accepted her invitation. During the past few months, she had been dating Eddie Murphy, the actor and comedian who'd recorded a couple of hit singles: 1985's "Party All the Time" (produced by Rick James) and the funky, Prince-like "Put Your Mouth On Me" that I had recently written and produced for him. Eddie was at the party, and his birthday gift to Whitney was a huge diamond ring that very nearly took her breath away.

All of us there had a fantastic time. A fabulous, buffet-style food spread, plenty of drink, excellent company, and, of course, great music—what more could we ask for? At one point in the evening, as "Just the Lonely Talking Again" rang out over the P.A., I enjoyed a slow dance with the birthday girl, during which she told me that

Michael Jackson had also been invited, but, unable to attend, he'd sent his pet chimpanzee Bubbles as a substitute. Personally, I never saw the chimp.

After our dance, while we sipped champagne, I took advantage of briefly having Whitney to myself by describing exactly how I felt about her unprecedented success.

"I'm so *proud* of you," I asserted, prompting her to laugh nervously, as if she was unsure where I was taking this.

"No, I'm *serious*," I persisted. "Look at what you've accomplished. Can you believe it? My beautiful Nippy, how great you are. You've changed the *whole game!*"

"How great *God* is for letting us do what we do," she replied, flashing her beautiful smile. I had never seen her more happy. What a contrast to my previous visit, when black clouds had appeared to engulf her home as well as her spirit. For now, those clouds had disappeared, and the Whitney we all knew and loved was radiant once again.

"You and Robyn should take a break at the Kona Village Resort," I told her, referring to the magnificent eighty-two-acre Polynesian beachfront property on the Big Island of Hawaii that Anukampa and I adored visiting. "It's so beautiful, so peaceful there, with *killer* food. You can unplug for a minute, quit the rat race, and get a cottage right on the ocean."

Which is precisely what happened. Robyn made all of the arrangements, and a short time later she and Whitney enjoyed a ten-day stayed at the resort. When they returned, Robyn told me, "You know what, it was the best thing that could have happened. All she did was rest. I'd bring her meals to the room and let her relax and look at the ocean."

=====

STILL HIGH ON THE outrageous, runaway success of Nippy's second album, I co-wrote five songs with Preston Glass for the follow-up. Excited about their prospects and eager for some feedback, I then sent Clive Davis the tracks that we recorded at Tarpan. All were rejected. It was, let me tell you, some wake-up call: a clear message that, despite my contributions to Whitney's studio-based achievements, I could forget about having any influence regarding the choice of material for her new record.

Perhaps the songs had already been selected, or our compositions didn't match Whitney's desired musical direction. Either way, having worked hard to come up with some soul-flavored ballads and up-tempo pop/R&B numbers that, we thought, would be ideally suited to Whitney's voice and her audience, we were very disappointed by how all of them were summarily dismissed. (I still have those backing tracks in the vaults.)

On the upside, I was asked to produce a half-dozen songs for the new album: the sensuous, midtempo "Feels So Good," "I Belong to You," and "Lover for Life"; the power ballad "All the Man That I Need"; the more sultry "Dancin' on the Smooth Edge"; and a cover of Steve Winwood's 1986 smash hit "Higher Love." I created backing tracks at Tarpan, working with my engineer David Frazer and a core band of guitarists, keyboard players, backing singers, and Kitty Beethoven performing the guide lead vocal while I played bass and drums.

My next stop was Right Track in New York to record Whitney. When we met there on the first day, she greeted me with a warm hug but appeared tired and didn't talk a whole lot. Fair enough. We all have our good days and bad days. I didn't give it much thought and kicked things off by running through the lyrics of "Feels So Good," so that she would know how I wanted to capture the song's romantic mood. Then, as usual, we recorded everything in sections, Whitney performing several takes with consummate ease before redoing certain parts according to my instructions. Still, I did notice that, instead of being her normal vibrant self, Nippy was all business.

Afterward, we chatted for a few minutes, and when she left, I began compiling the track with Lincoln Clapp. Following a good night's rest, I assumed, Whitney would return the next afternoon refreshed and raring to go. As usual, I kept working until well after midnight, at which point I returned with my brother, Kevin—who was my assistant on this project—to the Royalton Hotel. There, the next morning, I awoke to a disturbing call from my guru, Sri Chinmoy.

Just as Whitney sought God's guidance in her life, I prayed, meditated, and looked to my guru to keep me on the spiritual path. Sri Chinmoy and I would talk on the phone, and whenever I was in New York he'd invite me to come visit him in Queens. But on this occasion in early 1990, he had something else on his mind.

"Please watch out for Whitney Houston. I was meditating this morning, and something told me you must be very careful with her."

The two of us normally never talked about music or the people with whom I worked, so I took this unexpected warning very seriously.

"Okay," I responded, my voice rising in tone as if I were asking a question, inviting the guru to expand on what he'd just said.

"Something told me she's very troubled, very depressed, almost close to death."

"*Really?*" This shocked me.

"Something's not right."

It wasn't a long conversation, but it sure changed my whole perspective on Whitney. After I hung up the phone, I played a cassette of our previous day's work on "Feels So Good." As I began listening to her sing—"I can't control myself because only you can fulfill my every need, only you can save me . . ."—I became frightened. Would this love song be the last thing I'd ever work on with Nippy? I had noticed that she looked tired in the studio. Her youthful exuberance was missing, and it was something of an effort for her to act enthused about this new project. But I hadn't realized things might be *this* bad during a period when her career was still skyrocketing.

As soon as we hooked up at Right Track later that afternoon, I came straight to the point without actually telling her what the guru had said: "Is everything okay with you, Honey? I know you're tired, but I get the feeling something else is getting you down."

Something was. Opening up to me like I was her big brother, Whitney told me about her relationship with Eddie Murphy. Having hung out at Tarpan and around Hollywood with that multitalented guy, I knew he really had it down when it came to both the smooth talk and the sharp-assed street rap. Therefore, I could easily picture the scene Whitney now described to me: At the start of their brief relationship, he had held her hand while they stood in front of a mirror and told her to study their physical similarities. "Look at your face, now look at my face. Now imagine our faces together."

Sad but not crying, Whitney broke this down for me, so that I could understand what she had bought into—how perfect they looked together, how perfect they *were* together. Committing herself emotionally, she had fallen madly in love, only for Eddie to pull the plug, tell her it was over, and leave her devastated. Eddie was my friend, and because I didn't know the reasons for his sudden change of heart, I wasn't about to judge him. I had heard only one side of the story, and what happened between those two hot-blooded cats was part of the human experience, but it was still hard for me to see Whitney so vulnerable, so heartbroken. Which is why, trying to lighten the mood, I jokingly asked, "Do you want me to go kick his ass?"

"You really *do* love me, don't you?" she responded, smiling faintly through the sadness.

"*Yeah*, I love you."

Offering to kick Eddie's ass had triggered visible appreciation—street girl Nippy! I felt better after we talked. Sure, we'd often discussed the hardships of show business, but it's another thing confessing that you've been ditched by someone you love and don't know what to do about it. This was the first time we'd ever had a heart-to-heart of that depth about her personal life.

That having been said, there were still moments that day when she looked lost in thought, leading me to believe there was something else she didn't want to talk about. Whatever it was, the whole episode with Eddie had worn her out. Nevertheless, we did some work, adding the finishing touches to "Feels So Good," while I kept a close eye on her and got to grips with a project that was clearly taking this twenty-six-year-old idol of millions in a different musical direction.

When producing the song's backing track at Tarpan, I had drawn on the sound and energy of Marvin Gaye's "Sexual Healing," incorporating the configuration of rhythms that were a part of his genius. The demo alone had informed me we were going more R&B, more ghetto jukebox, with a long intro providing space for vocal ad-libs before the number really begins. No one, Clive included, had told me, "You've got to make a blacker record," but the song itself strongly suggested that. Was this a wise decision? I wouldn't go there. I wasn't being paid to offer my opinions; I was being hired to do my very best with the material I was given. If we were going more for the hood, that was fine with me.

We were now dealing less with a song than with a sexual, sensual R&B groove, and the same applied to the next track that Whitney overdubbed, "I Belong to You." Again, this had a long intro and Marvin Gaye vibe, and it called for the kind of laid-back, understated vocal that some listeners may mistakenly assume would be relatively easy for a singer of Whitney Houston's talent. It's actually harder to sing softly in tune for any length of time—not only is it extremely taxing, but it requires a lot of air on the vocal chords to achieve that breathy sound.

At this stage of Whitney's career, there hadn't been any vocal degeneration because she still had a way of recovering from all the wear and tear. "I managed to sleep eight or nine hours," she would often tell me. At other times, she'd say, "You know I said I was coming in at four? Make it five. I need some more sleep." That was the first time I really understood how important sleep is for a singer. Those eight or nine hours *heal*.

For "I Belong to You," Whitney the actress had to be called upon to convincingly deliver the song's suggestively upbeat message, proclaiming, "I've been to the bottom, now I'm back on top, when I'm feelin' the rhythm as we start to rock . . ." This was hardly representative of where her life was at. Regardless, it was incredibly important that Whitney artistically identify with the sentiment to capture the right feel. Accordingly, we ran through the lyrics to ease her into the process—discussing their meaning to break down the emotions—before she began singing.

Nippy could have sung the phone book if she'd wanted, but to sell the record she had to reach inside herself and find the part that matched the mood of the song. Despite all of her adult problems, her childlike spirit enabled her to believe in the message of these songs. So, we settled into our routine to get in the right frame of mind: I played the piano, and she warmed up with "Alfie" and "Walk On By." As I've said before, Whitney never needed to warm up her voice when it was time to record. We'd just roll tape and *bam*! However, the emotional warm-up was really important.

That girl had a natural sense of rhythm, a rhythm that helped her records become smashes, more so, even, than the songs' melodies. Like many truly great R&B singers—Marvin, Prince, Michael, Stevie—her phrasing was spot-on, and that's because she had rhythm in her *soul*. Still, for me, what made Nippy's performance of "I Belong to You" so touching was that I knew she had been emotionally crushed by a failed relationship and was mentally and physically exhausted. It was written all over her beautiful face.

For that reason, I fought my natural instinct to work at a fast pace on the third album, making a concerted effort to slow things down and give her what Al Jarreau would refer to as *more ramp*. This meant rewinding the tape farther than usual when Whitney was going to punch in a segment—redoing a line, word, or syllable for insertion into the main vocal—so that she'd have a longer time to recapture the mood. And I also gave her more leeway in general, occasionally suggesting, "If you don't want to record today, we don't have to record today. Come back tomorrow." Although I don't recall Nippy taking me up on that offer, it helped assure her that I was on her side.

Leniency was the name of the game, yet some things never changed. We still had our little contest, doing twenty push-ups a day. Robyn attended every session over the course of about two weeks, and John and Cissy Houston would drop by the studio to check on their daughter. A new face was Whitney's friend and sometime-backing vocalist, gospel singer BeBe Winans, who would come in toward the end of her session and then, for some unknown reason, want to stay afterward, sleeping on the backroom couch. Not a problem. I bought him a blanket—named, naturally, BeBe's Blanket—and he'd sleep there while Lincoln Clapp and I were compiling the track.

In his role as my assistant, my brother, Kevin, would visit the studio to make sure everything was running smoothly. He was there when we were tracking the vocal for "All the Man That I Need," and he happened to have a little photo of himself in a bathing suit, looking at the beach. Kevin's a handsome guy, the shot of him gazing at the water was taken from behind, and Whitney was more than a little impressed when she saw it.

"What's the big deal?" I asked, feeling a little embarrassed by her blatant interest in my own brother.

"Look at him!" she replied. "Look at how he's put together!"

Kevin and I laughed it off. But then, when Nippy began recording, she stared straight at him, inspired by that picture, and she switched gears. Whereas she had still been finding her way through the fog while tracking "I Belong to You," she emerged from the fog on "All the Man That I Need," exuding the same energy that had been present on "One Moment in Time."

Written by Dean Pitchford and Michael Gore, "All the Man That I Need" had previously been recorded without much success by R&B/house singer Linda Clifford and soul/disco group Sister Sledge. Now, after going down the ghetto jukebox path with "Feels So Good" and "I Belong to You," Whitney and I found ourselves back on home turf with this stirring power ballad, not only doing what we'd done on the second album, but doing it even better. There were more small ingredients in the gumbo to subtly improve the flavor, with synthesized strings and vibes at the beginning of the song providing a celestial atmosphere to pave the way for Whitney to make her grand entrance by descending from the heavens.

I was always searching for elements to acquire that feel on her records—the angel visiting us from a higher plane—and in this case Walter Afanasieff and I had experimented a fair bit at Tarpan by messing around on a synth while asking, "What does this do?" and "What does that do?" As with every song, we had to build "All the Man That I Need" element-by-element virtually from scratch—a hit-and-miss process that Quincy Jones likens to painting a 747 with a Q-tip. It's so true. *Here's a little Q-tip, now go paint that big-ass airplane!*

In the case of "All the Man That I Need," the intro was inspired by the soaring strings and choir at the start of Johnny Mathis's hit 1958 recording of "A Certain Smile." That intro helped key the rest of "All the Man That I Need," reenergizing Nippy and providing her with all the inspiration that *she* needed to take the song to another level once she transitioned from the delicate verse to the dynamic chorus.

Meanwhile, timpani delivered the kind of power you typically hear in a James Bond theme. Musically speaking, this type of song always has to make a dramatic statement to become a hit, and the most dramatic of all takes place via the key modulation after Kenny G's sax solo, when the chorus shifts up an octave. The vocal fireworks capture Whitney Houston at her greatest. And I was also proud of the call-and-response between her and the choir of multitracked backing singers.

Whitney's happiness is clearly audible on the record. Yet, following an ecstatic "Whoo!" her voice drops out for the final twenty-five seconds of the song, leaving the backing singers alone with Mike Gibbs's sweeping orchestration.

"Nippy, my love, you've sung so much on this ending, if you sing any more it's going to explode," I explained to her when we were dealing with the end section. "So, just cut it off."

"How do I do that?"

"Imagine this is a live show. Go 'Whoo!' almost like you're going to drop the mic and walk offstage."

This was another change from the second album, on which I may well have had her sing all the way to the fade. The musical maturation process had taught me you've got to know when to stop. Whitney got that, too. Instead of wailing more, why not let the majesty of the orchestration carry the song to its conclusion?

"Wow, that's *different*! I love it!"

We'd never done that before. It was about being more discerning, about not overdoing things, about creating a track that you can listen to over and over again without feeling beaten up and tired of it. *Less is sometimes more.*

"Dancin' on the Smooth Edge," written by David Lasley and Robbie Long, was a ballad in a different vein, with a sophisticated arrangement and a sensuous vocal that echoed the Bacharach/

David—related recordings of Dionne. However, even though I embellished it with elements of the Isley Brothers, Stevie Wonder, and the ghetto outhouse, it wasn't a song conceived in the hood. The title sounds as if it's meant to be derived from there, but it isn't a black term. I'm not even sure what it means. What is the "smooth edge"—a razor blade? As usual, Whitney did an amazing job—vamping, harmonizing, and singing mainly in higher, lighter "head" voice.

Nippy actually selected the next song we worked on: a souped-up, funky cover of Steve Winwood's R&B chart-topper "Higher Love," which he'd co-written with Will Jennings and recorded with Chaka Khan on backing vocals. Our version, a solid groove that was over five minutes long, featured Whitney in fifth gear for a good portion of that time—she was rocking so hard. The whole thing became so spiritual, so immersed in gospel and the church; it just kept getting better and better and better. I was grateful that I had cut a lengthy backing track for the song at Tarpan. My drumming bracketed a lot of intervals, and I had to put in a fair amount of work teaching Nippy those breaks, since they were slightly different from the Winwood record. To her credit, she was in the zone and got them down perfectly.

Talk about turning things around. Just a week earlier, Whitney had been under a black cloud and finding it difficult to get fired up about *anything*, but the music was obviously providing her with a much-needed diversion and a temporary escape from all the heartache. She was on a hot streak in the studio, and we had just one more song to work on together—the one that, when cutting the backing track at Tarpan, had driven David Frazer, the musicians, and me totally crazy.

Penned by soul singer/composer/producer Sam Dees, "Lover for Life" was dubbed "The Little Demo that Could" by assistant engineer David Chappelle because, as far as we were concerned, it was broken. The bass drum pattern on Dees's demo was in a different time signature (5/4, meaning five beats to the bar) than the other instruments and the rest of the kit (all of which were 4/4, meaning four beats to the bar). Consequently, that bass drum wasn't synchronized with everything else. Assuming this was a mistake, we changed its time signature to 4/4 when cutting the track onto which Whitney would overdub her vocals. However, after taking a listen, Clive rejected it—"No, it's not close enough to the demo."

When first assigning me the material that I was going to produce for the third album, he had told me, "Pray, meditate, go to the top of the mountain if you have to. Just do whatever it takes to make these songs strong." I therefore made some small changes to the "Lover for Life" arrangement, rerecorded certain parts, and sent him that version. Again, he rejected it: "The feel just isn't the same."

As suggested by Clive, version three was in the vein of Anita Baker's smooth R&B hit "Caught Up in the Rapture," featuring a more jazz-based groove. This was a fairly radical change, but when he listened to the cassette that I handed him in his bungalow at the Beverly Hills Hotel, he still didn't like what he heard: "No, no, no, it's *too* jazzy. Listen to the demo again. You've got to hear what *I'm* hearing . . ."

I must have listened to that demo fifty zillion times, and I still didn't have a clue what he wanted. Clive's passionate about the music, but he now appeared to be suffering from a severe case of *demo-itis*. After four weeks of working on the track, I was exhausted and at my wits' end. Still, I wasn't mad at him; he was my partner and my love for him was what motivated me to achieve the results he desired.

"You can't be talking about the bass drum in 5/4," I said.

"What do you mean?"

"How it keeps moving about."

"Maybe that's what it is. *I* don't know."

"I tell you what, I'm going to cut this thing note-for-note, just like the demo."

That's what I did, copying "The Little Demo that Could" right down to that bass drum's strange 5/4 time signature. When Clive heard it, he was enraptured; forefinger on lips, eyes half-closed, swept away to Shangri-La.

"I feel like I'm floating," he murmured.

"You're floating because it's five bars against four," I responded almost in disbelief.

"Whatever. I'm floating."

"That's really what you *want*?"

"Yeah, I'm floating."

"*Okay . . .*"

I was amazed, but Clive loved every little nuance. The track with the bass drum doing its own mindless thing somehow had the right feel to realize his musical fantasy of sitting in a small, dark, intimate piano bar where the spotlight is focused on a sultry female singer. He'd often describe that image to me when explaining what he envisioned for one of the slow, sensuous songs that he had selected for Whitney. When she subsequently delivered the desired "Lover for Life" vocal at Right Track—effortlessly replicating Sam Dees's improvisations while adding her own, unaffected by the erratic bass drum—the picture was complete. As was my two weeks' work with her this time around.

The third album would be titled *I'm Your Baby Tonight* after the lead single, written and produced by Babyface and L.A. Reid. Considering that Clive had previously told me he didn't want any songs with the word *baby*—he probably thought it sounded too clichéd—this was quite a switcheroo. But it would turn out to be the least of the surprises when I finally got to hear the finished record.

"With 'I'm Every Woman,' Whitney was doing voice replacement at the film studio for *The Bodyguard*, posing for publicity shots, and doing so many other things at the same time that, when she came in to record her vocal, she said, 'Okay, I've got two and a half hours to do this song.' However, even though she may have been worn out and beaten up by her schedule, she still delivered. The work was intense, and she just blasted through it. Whereas performing in front of a large concert audience energizes an artist, the same can hardly be said for a recording studio—it normally takes time to get to the level that's reached when singing to twenty thousand people. But Whitney was able to get there right away. She was really easy to record, and for me it didn't feel like work—it was more like *wow*! No preparation, and yet there it all was, just perfect."

—DAVID FRAZER, recording engineer

CHAPTER SIX

RENEWED LIFE,
RENEWED ENERGY

T THE START OF THE 1990S, Whitney was no longer the rising star reaching for the top. Globally acclaimed, fabulously wealthy, and massively, *massively* successful, she had already achieved what she'd originally set out to do, and with the impending release of her third album, there were now other up-and-comers aspiring to her throne.

Chief among them was Mariah Carey, a nineteen-year-old New Yorker with an opera-singing mother and a phenomenal voice. Tommy Mottola, the head of Sony Music Entertainment, had signed her to the company's Columbia Records label in the hope of rivaling Sire Records' pop icon Madonna and Arista's vocal megastar Whitney Houston. To that end, in 1988 Mottola began laying the groundwork for Mariah's self-titled first album. Keen for it to largely feature her co-compositions with Ben Margulies, he nevertheless balked at the idea of them producing the record on their own and recruited Ric Wake, Rhett Lawrence, and me to help out in that department as well as with some songwriting.

Rhett and I co-produced Mariah's chart-topping debut single "Vision of Love"—written by Ben and Mariah—and, in addition to producing and co-writing the chart-topping "I Don't Wanna Cry" with her, I also co-produced "There's Got to Be a Way" with Ric. Of course, Mariah knew all about the work I'd done with Whitney. During one of the March 1990 sessions to track her vocals in New York, she was just dying to hear the new recordings that Nippy and I had collaborated on for the yet-to-be-released *I'm Your Baby Tonight* album. I didn't really want to play her anything, but Mariah was such a fan, and she was so persistent: "Please, *please* let me just hear something of it."

Figuring she'd soon be hearing it anyway, I played her little bits of "I Belong to You" and "Feels So Good"—just enough for her to go, "Oh . . . my . . . *God*!"

"Is my stuff anywhere near as good as this?" she asked, as if she was inviting me to tell her some awful truth.

"Your stuff is *fantastic*," I reassured her. "But it's different, so you can't compare the two."

Artistic insecurity—Whitney wasn't immune to it either. After Mariah subsequently became huge (thanks to her first four singles topping the Billboard Hot 100), I heard from Robyn Crawford that Nippy got mad because I had given her sound to Mariah. That just wasn't true. Yes, some of the same machines were employed for both of their records, but the songs were different, the approach was different, the vocalizing was different, and they each had their own sound. Still, what this whole episode demonstrated to me was the effect that Whitney Houston had on *everyone*, whether it was a super-talented newcomer like Mariah Carey or the legendary Queen of Soul, Miss Aretha Franklin.

On Saint Patrick's Day, my wife, Anukampa, and I attended That's What Friends Are For: Arista Records 15th Anniversary Concert, an all-star AIDS benefit staged at Radio City Music Hall. Whitney opened the six-hour show with "How Will I Know" and slayed the crowd. Afterward, there was a dinner at Tavern on the Green in Central Park. Although the restaurant was packed to capacity and we didn't stay long, I managed to have a chat with Nippy, praising her performance and discussing the show in general.

On one level, I felt confident being around her because of our work together, but on another I have to say it was also a mind-blowing experience for me every time. Despite my musical involvement with many major artists down the years, I've never lost the tendency to indulge in a little hero worship. Therefore, once Whitney had reached that hallowed status of the true superstar and cultural icon, being in her presence and engaging in conversation absolutely delighted me.

I admired Whitney's talent and beauty the way people worship Elvis Presley. Given that dynamic, our intimate conversations—how much she needed affection, what kind of men turned her on—were always initiated by Nippy. They had to be. They had to take place at a time when she was in the right mood to let it all down. "Oh, you're in town? Come over," she might say to me if I happened to be in New York. It was never preplanned. Whether the talk was lighthearted or deep, I always felt blessed to have this kind of relationship and to be invited into her inner sanctum of family, friends, and associates—not just to the studio where I was expected to be the magician pulling the rabbit out of a hat.

On April 16, Whitney called while I was still working with Mariah and invited me to her home in Mendham, New Jersey. Anukampa accompanied me—by now, she and Whitney were also good friends—and subsequently recorded the occasion in her diary.

> We arrive at the house in the evening, around 9:30 PM. Whitney greets us with a big smile at the front door, dressed casually in black tights and a pullover sweater. She escorts us to the kitchen where she asks her assistant to get us some food that she made specifically for us. We all relax and eat, chatting and laughing. Narada and Whitney go have a private chat about the music and a few minutes later return to the living room area. We continue our conversation and cover a variety of subjects: music, sex, age, God, relationships, movies, etc. Whitney is very energetic and is having a good time. She loves to talk, and she loves to laugh. She is a good mimic of other people . . . She mentions that she misses Eddie Murphy.

About three months later, Arista sent me the *I'm Your Baby Tonight* running order. "All the Man That I Need," "Lover for Life," and "I Belong to You" were on the album; "Feels So Good," "Dancin' on the Smooth Edge," and "Higher Love" were not. Of course, I was disappointed to discover that half of the tracks I had produced were missing. It was unusual for the work that I did on *any* project to go unused. These omissions, coupled with the rejection of the five songs that Preston Glass and I had originally written for the album, were a considerable snub given the success of my previous collaborations with Whitney.

Don't get me wrong: Having three tracks on an album by an artist of Nippy's caliber was still a tremendous honor, and I was *very* proud to have anything to do with her whatsoever. That was on the human level. But on the professional one I wasn't used to having my work discarded like this, especially after Clive had approved the recordings.

The final lineup of contributors to *I'm Your Baby Tonight* was impressive, including L.A. Reid and Babyface, who produced four of their own compositions. No doubt about it, they were hot at that time, and teaming Whitney with them—as well as with Luther Vandross and Stevie Wonder—was an astute way of trying to heighten her appeal within the black marketplace. Whether it did the same for her global popularity and ultimately benefited her career is open to question, but I, apparently, was no longer the flavor of the day and that wasn't a good feeling.

"Feels So Good" would end up on the B side of the album's lead single, "I'm Your Baby Tonight," and "Dancin' on the Smooth Edge" would be relegated to the flip side of "All the Man That I Need." However, Whitney's dynamic, *incredible* cover of Steve Winwood's "Higher Love"—a song that she herself had asked to record—was only ever issued as a bonus track on the Japanese version of *I'm Your Baby Tonight*. Everywhere else, it remains unreleased. And it's still *smoking*, one of her greatest vocal performances.

I wasn't about to call Clive and bitch, "Why didn't you use all of my songs, man?" I certainly wasn't going to call Whitney to complain about it. That would have made me look stupid. Besides, it was too late to change what had already been done. Whenever I saw Nippy, I wanted to be on my best behavior: "Hey, it's all cool! You cool? *I'm* cool . . ." So, that was my attitude when, on October 23, 1990, a couple of weeks before the album's release, Anukampa and I attended Clive's listening party at the Beverly Hills Hotel.

To be honest, in light of what had happened with the record, I wasn't really feeling this event, but I obviously had to go.

It's standard practice for a record label to stage a gathering for members of the press to preview a major new album just before its release. This enables the publicists to do their job: schmoozing the journalists, building anticipation, and providing plenty of positive information in the hope of encouraging positive reviews. In this case, the private and exclusive listening session was also for those involved in the making of Whitney's new record. Because it hadn't been produced by one person, there were several of us who hadn't yet heard the finished product.

The hotel conference room in which the session took place was pretty small, capable of accommodating about a hundred people, and when Anukampa and I arrived it was probably half full. Arista's executive vice president, Roy Lott, was the first person to greet us, and he seemed happy enough to see me. However, probably guessing my unusually sedate demeanor meant I wasn't thrilled to be there, he also looked jittery and nervous. The same went for Clive. No one knew how anyone was going to react to *I'm Your Baby Tonight,* and instead of confidence filling the air as it had at the listening party for the previous album, there was a general sense of anxiety. Everyone seemed to be sweating bullets over this record's chances of being another smash, and Stevie Wonder showing up late with the tape of his duet with Whitney hardly helped calm executive nerves.

So many people were squeezed into the small room—including friends and acquaintances of Whitney, such as Barry Manilow and Maria Shriver—that it was soon uncomfortably crowded, and I felt increasingly uncomfortable about staying. Just before the program was about to begin, I walked up to Anukampa and said I wanted to go. "With the last album I felt like a Super Bowl champion," I told her, "but now I just have a small piece of the pie."

Standing nearby, Roy Lott overheard this and immediately went into a panic. "Narada, you can't leave!" he asserted in a loud whisper. "It'll look *really bad,* and Whitney will be *really upset!*"

Before I could answer, he began jabbering to my wife: "Anukampa, he *must stay*! He doesn't want to piss off Clive!"

All I had wanted was to quietly disappear, but Roy was now making such a fuss that I reluctantly acquiesced: "Okay, okay, I'll stay, I'll stay."

Unlike many listening parties where the invitees are encouraged to stand and mingle, this session was a sit-down affair. Several rows of folding chairs crammed together added to the stifling atmosphere. Nevertheless, we took our assigned seats in the front row and were joined there by Eddie Murphy, who had called me beforehand to ask for the address. Even though Eddie and Whitney were no longer an item, he had still been invited, and I was glad about that. Like us, however, he ended up sitting in the worst possible place—right next to the speakers—and as we soon discovered, this wasn't only a listening party, but also a viewing party.

Clive introduced the video for "I'm Your Baby Tonight." Although I thought it was well made—with Whitney portraying iconic figures such as Marlene Dietrich, Audrey Hepburn, and even all three members of the Supremes—it was also noticeable that she had more edge than in previous years, her apparent innocence replaced by street-girl attitude. This may have been entertaining had the music not been cranked up way too loud, to the point where Eddie, Anukampa, and I were all cringing at the distorted sound. Things didn't get much better after that.

For me, the album lacked consistency due to its eclectic, uneasy mixture of pop, R&B, and new jack swing (a fusion of urban contemporary R&B with the rhythms and samples of hip-hop and dance-pop that was then sweeping the black club scene). The result was *something for everyone* that fell somewhere in between. Still, perhaps the biggest problem from my perspective was that a lot of the material just wasn't as strong as on Whitney's first two records.

Following the near-hour-long listening session, Nippy took to the stage and thanked everyone for attending. Afterward, I gave her a quick hug and said, "Well done, my love," before Anukampa and I strolled out to the parking lot and then drove to Eddie Murphy's house in Malibu. Formerly owned by Cher, the Egyptian-style home boasted massive gates in front of a curved, stone driveway while an atrium with a fully retractable glass roof revealed the nighttime L.A. sky at the push of a button. "Whose place do you think is better?" he quipped with that trademark mischievous look in his eye. "Whitney's or mine?"

Eddie was really buzzing, cracking jokes in his quick-fire fashion as we ate pizza in the kitchen. Afterward, we spoke privately in his bedroom, standing next to the big jukebox that I'd bought for him when we'd worked together. Eddie said only a few words about Whitney, but I could tell there was sadness.

"It wasn't good the way that whole thing ended," he remarked quietly.

"It really screwed Whitney up," I replied.

"Yeah, I know," he said. "I really didn't mean for that to happen."

That was it. Two guys sharing a brief, private moment. Then we moved on to other things. I'd made my point, but it wasn't my place to say anything else.

I'm Your Baby Tonight was released on November 6, 1990, and quickly became an international hit. However, it didn't sell as well as Nippy's first two albums. *Whitney* had topped the charts in five countries, *Whitney Houston* in a dozen, but this third one didn't match that feat anywhere, including the United States, where it peaked at number three on the Billboard 200, spent twenty-two weeks in the Top Ten, and remained on the chart for fifty-one weeks. At the same time, topping *Billboard*'s R&B chart for eight weeks helped it become 1991's number one album in that category.

"Ms. Houston's voice has never sounded so rhythmically elastic, more shivery with power and assurance," Stephen Holden wrote in the *New York Times,* while noting, "the exigencies of pop fashion have required the cultivation of a different voice—a tougher, streetwise personality that seems even farther removed from the church."

David Browne of *Entertainment Weekly* agreed: "*Baby* adheres doggedly to one agenda: to prove Houston is a get-down, funky human being who can party with the best of them."

On the singles front, the title track and "All the Man That I Need" became, respectively, Whitney's eighth and ninth recordings to hit the top spot on the Billboard Hot 100. In his *Rolling Stone* review, James Hunter asserted that "Houston and Walden control 'All the Man That I Need,' an outsize ballad about poverty and damaged self-regard, so expertly that the song, with its effective whiff of a Spanish guitar, stages undeniable pop drama."

In the meantime, Nippy's breathtaking, soul-flavored rendition of "The Star-Spangled Banner" at Super Bowl XXV in Tampa, Florida, on January 27, 1991—wonderfully arranged by Rickey Minor—was issued the following month and peaked at number six on the U.S. chart. The Whitney Houston Foundation for Children donated all of her proceeds from the record's sales to the American Red Cross Gulf Crisis Fund, which, together with the royalties donated by Arista and the Bertelsmann Music Group, raised more than half a million dollars for U.S. soldiers, their families, and victims of the Gulf War.

This theme continued on March 31, when Whitney performed in front of a select audience of thirty-one thousand military personnel and their relatives at the Naval Station in Norfolk, Virginia, to honor those returning from the war. Broadcast live on HBO (which unscrambled the signal so that the program could be seen in fifty-three million cable-equipped households), *Welcome Home Heroes with Whitney Houston* was her first solo concert to be televised, and it featured a setlist very similar to the one used on her I'm Your Baby Tonight World Tour. Having commenced with a couple of gigs in Yokohama, Japan, on March 14 and 15, the tour continued in North America from April 18 through August 17, before sweeping through Europe until the first week of October.

At a time when a global financial crisis hit ticket sales and a number of major artists were forced to cancel their live shows, Nippy suffered the same fate. Attendance at a number of venues was low, poor sales resulted in the cancellation of several dates, and she ended her Canadian tour early due to a throat problem. Still, despite criticism from some quarters that dancing, large-scale lighting, and multiple costume changes were taking precedence over the music, she broke her own record of playing nine straight nights at London's Wembley Arena back in 1988 by going one better there in September of '91.

The shows now featured funkier arrangements of Nippy's up-tempo material; several of her popular love songs were merged into a "Love Medley," so that she had more time for the new jack swing numbers; and rappers performed "How Will I Know" verses, while embellishing other favorites with shouts of "Yo Whitney!" This was a whole new slant to both the music and her image at a time when the more black-oriented singles still being released off *I'm Your Baby Tonight* were producing diminishing returns. "Miracle" reached number nine on the Billboard Hot 100 and "My Name Is Not Susan" number twenty, whereas both "I Belong to You" and "We Didn't Know" would actually fail to chart.

At some shows, another pointer to the future lay in Whitney dedicating a beautiful medley of "All the Man That I Need" and Billie Holiday's "Lover Man" to her *own man*. Step forward new jack swing pioneer Mr. Bobby Brown! After Nippy's breakup with Eddie, she and Bobby had begun dating. By the end of 1991, she was heavily preoccupied with him, and I saw less and less of her on a social basis.

She and I did get together for my fortieth birthday party on April 23, 1992, when a small group of us—including Anukampa and Whitney's publicist, Regina Brown—had dinner at an Indian restaurant in midtown Manhattan. The drinks flowed, we all got a little tipsy, and there was plenty of joking and laughter. The main thing I remember about that night is how Nippy didn't hold back when saying how she'd had enough of bowing to record company demands, as well as the publicists, tour managers, and anyone else whom she perceived as not being concerned about the toll that their pressure was taking on her.

"You know how hard I work."

"I do, I do."

"Yeah, well, I didn't get to this position so that I still can't have any time to myself. I'm not gonna take their bullshit anymore."

Nippy wasn't feeling down; she was having fun, letting loose with friends and intent on keeping things that way. This was at a time when her relationship with Bobby was on the up and up. Whenever I saw them together—holding hands and whispering affectionately while gazing into each other's eyes—they both looked really happy and totally in love.

Bobby and Whitney were married at her New Jersey home on July 18, 1992. After learning about the wedding via a TV news report, I never asked why I hadn't been invited. Instead, when Nippy called a couple of months later, asking me to produce a song for the soundtrack of *The Bodyguard*—the film in which she made her acting debut alongside Kevin Costner—I said, "Of course I will." I was, quite honestly, happy and honored that she still wanted to work with me.

Until that phone call, I didn't know a whole lot about the movie—no one tells you much about anything in our business unless you're involved. Still, as the album's executive producer, Whitney now had control over the choice of material, and the number she wanted me to cut was a cover of "I'm Every Woman." Written by the husband-and-wife team of Nickolas Ashford and Valerie Simpson, this had been a 1978 disco hit for Chaka Khan whom Nippy idolized.

"I've always loved the song," she subsequently explained. "I love Chaka and I admire the work of Nick Ashford and Valerie Simpson. It's got a lot of energy, a lot of soul, a lot of good feeling." Coupling Whitney's talent, enthusiasm, and incredible sense of rhythm with that song's dynamic qualities was a tantalizing proposition. The first thing I therefore did before laying down the backing track at Tarpan was study the current crop of dance records to make sure I was in the flow of where things were at and where they might be going. Trends change quickly within that genre, and I didn't want our record to sound dated.

To that end, whereas the original version produced by Arif Mardin had immediately commenced with disco strings setting the pace and the tone, I decided that Whitney's recording should have a little more light and shade. This meant a slow and sensuous first minute to showcase the beauty of her voice before really picking up the tempo with machine drums and classic synth strings—using the original string lines that were so much a part of the song—while adding a little guitar and some inside funk inspired by the top four or five recent club records. This would give the whole thing a contemporary feel—disco with powerful new flavors.

When, in mid-October, Whitney arrived at Hollywood's Ocean Way Recording on Sunset Boulevard to track her vocal in the facility's back room, the first thing she said to me was, "I'm *so* in love with Bobby." She certainly looked radiant. Nearly five months pregnant, Nippy was a little fuller in the face, but that angel face *glowed*. When I touched her belly to feel the baby kick, she kept going on and on about how much she was in love with Bobby. "I'm so happy I found him. I've finally found true love." Without me even asking, that's something she really wanted me to know, so I took her comments at face value and thought *good for you*. Renewed life, renewed energy.

Being that "I'm Every Woman" was a song that Whitney had chosen—not Clive, not anyone else—she really threw herself into the recording and had a definite idea of how she wanted it to turn out. After I'd put my mack hand down in terms of the track, she put her mack hand down in terms of the singing. What she did adhered closely to Chaka Khan's original arrangement, and she let me coach her to make sure she paid due homage. However, whereas I'd normally be the one to tell Nippy where we needed some more harmonizing, she was now guiding me, determined to do justice to the song by making every harmony as good as—if not even better than—Chaka's. She had razor-laser focus, and it made me happy to see Whitney so excited, so bubbly about something.

"Does it need another harmony here?" she might ask, to which I'd invariably reply, "Try it." Then, once she'd added the part, I would say, "Great, double it."

Whitney stacked all of her own parts with so much dynamism, as if to say, "Chaka, you gave us the blueprint. Here it is with new energy."

At one point, there was a knock on the control room door, and after the assistant engineer answered it, he said, "It's Natalie Cole."

"Tell her to come in!" I replied. I was a big fan of Natalie, as well as of her father Nat, so it was great to see how excited *she* was to come in and watch Whitney sing. What she saw was some hot rocking from a woman with a baby inside her. *Damn!* And she was also impressed by how hard Whitney worked on getting some of those high harmonies. Of course, I normally wouldn't allow people into the studio when Nippy was recording, but we were both cool with the idea of having music royalty bless the room in the form of Natalie Cole.

Whitney recorded all of her parts for "I'm Every Woman" in a single three-hour session—including her acknowledgment of "Chaka Khan. Chaka *Khan!*" toward the end of the song. I then took the tape back to Tarpan and, with David Frazer, compiled the best parts into the finished performance. David Cole and Robert Clivillés, partners in the hip-hop/dance-pop-based C+C Music

Factory, subsequently remixed the song that landed on the album and was released as a single. I thought they did a great job.

The Whitney I saw on that day at Ocean Way Recording is the Whitney I'd like to remember. Just like in the "I'm Every Woman" video that she shot a couple of weeks later—featuring cameos by Chaka, Valerie, Cissy, and the members of R&B/hip-hop/new jack swing trio TLC, and ending with Nippy showing off her sizeable tummy bump—she was ecstatic, effervescent, full of life, on top of her game, embracing the future. It was as if Heaven's light was shining down upon her, yet what none of us could have predicted was what that future would bring.

"Perhaps because it was the first song that he'd recorded with Whitney, Narada always appeared to be touched by her performance of 'How Will I Know.' Well, for '**Look Into Your Heart**'—which turned out to be the last track they'd ever work on together—he told her, 'Remember the beginning of "How Will I Know," where you came out so powerful on that first line, "There's a *boy* . . ." Do the same for this song: "If you look into your heart . . ."' Narada wanted that same kind of fire, and after Whitney produced it on the first take, he smiled big, as if to say, *That's what I'm talking about.* Aretha Franklin had recorded the original version of 'Look Into Your Heart,' and when Narada asked Whitney, 'What does this song mean to you?' she said, 'It's a very personal lyric that Aretha interpreted and I want to make sure I keep that integrity.' Narada told her, 'Then look into *your* heart,' and she did. While I was impressed by how at ease and down to earth Whitney was, the voice coming back through the studio monitors was just phenomenal."

—PRESTON GLASS, associate producer

CHAPTER SEVEN

A CHARGE OF
ELECTRICITY

F OLLOWING THE NOVEMBER 17, 1992, release of *The Bodyguard: Original Soundtrack Album* and the film itself a week later, Whitney entered a new phase of her career: one that would see her focus more on movies and less on making records.

A romantic thriller, *The Bodyguard* featured Nippy as a singer named Rachel Marron who, stalked by a hit man and a crazed fan, receives protection from former Secret Service agent Frank Farmer (Kevin Costner). Rachel and Frank eventually fall for one another, and in that regard Lawrence Kasdan's screenplay and Mick Jackson's direction broke down an important social barrier by taking interracial love for granted rather than making an issue out of it.

The film received mixed reviews from critics, who, in some cases, derided the "cheesy" plot and lack of chemistry between the co-stars. However, it was massively popular at the box office, raking in more than $121 million in the United States and over $400 million worldwide, making it the second-highest-grossing movie of 1992 and one of the one hundred top-grossing movies ever up until that time. Consequently, the album—for which Whitney recorded six of the twelve tracks, while once again executive producing with Clive Davis—was also a smash hit, spending a combined twenty weeks at number one on the Billboard 200, while topping the charts in no fewer than sixteen other countries. Selling more than 45 million copies worldwide, *The Bodyguard* would become the best-selling soundtrack album of all time.

Meanwhile, the record's David Foster–produced lead single— a stunning, soul-laced interpretation by Whitney of the Dolly Parton ballad "I Will Always Love You"—spent a record-breaking fourteen weeks atop the Billboard Hot 100, reached number one in fifteen other countries, and became Nippy's most successful single ever. What's more, it was only halfway through its run at number one in the United States when "I'm Every Woman" was released on January 2, 1993. Outperforming the Chaka Khan original, this rose to number four on the Billboard Hot 100 and was also a Top Five hit in the UK.

That July, Whitney kicked off a world tour that would continue until late November 1994, and during that stretch of time she actually made a return trip to Tarpan. This was for a song that she really wanted to record for the all-star album *A Tribute to Curtis Mayfield*. I was one of the producers of *New World Order*, the record that the soul/R&B/funk legend had begun working on when, in 1990, stage lighting equipment fell on him during an outdoor concert and paralyzed him from the waist down. Afterward, unable to play the guitar,

Curtis had been forced to record his vocals, line by line, while lying on his back on the floor of the studio. It was really, really sad. This final album wouldn't be released until 1997, two years before his death, but in the meantime, in late 1993, I was also involved with the tribute record.

Amid a lineup that included, among others, Aretha Franklin, Eric Clapton, Gladys Knight, Bruce Springsteen, B.B. King, Rod Stewart, Phil Collins, and Stevie Wonder performing Curtis's songs, I produced Whitney singing "Look Into Your Heart," Tevin Campbell's version of "Keep On Pushin'," and my own performance of "(Don't Worry) If There's a Hell Below, We're All Going to Go." Nippy's choice of number had originally been recorded by Aretha for her album *Sparkle*, the soundtrack that Curtis wrote and produced for the 1976 movie of the same name starring Irene Cara.

Clive had nothing to do with Whitney's recording; it was something that she and I alone agreed she should do, and, as usual, she tracked her vocal in the space of three hours at Tarpan. What an incredible performance—full of soul, energy, and Aretha-type grit. Yet, back then, in light of what Nippy and I had already achieved in the studio, we regarded it as just another session. Had someone told me it would be the last time we'd ever work together, I would have never believed it.

A few months later, on March 1, 1994, we saw each other at the Grammy Awards. Nippy was radiant in a long, figure-hugging white dress and—after a quick costume change following her performance of "I Will Always Love You"—a stunning metallic, geometrically-patterned, full-length dress. She won three times that night, scooping up Record of the Year (with David Foster); Best Female Pop Vocal Performance for "I Will Always Love You"; and Album of the

Year with Babyface, L.A. Reid, BeBe Winans, David Foster, David Cole, Robert Clivillés, and me for the *Bodyguard* soundtrack.

Right before we went onstage to receive the award, a beaming Nippy grabbed me and cried, "We did it; we did it! I'm so excited!"

"Yes, honey, *we did it!*" I replied as we enjoyed a quick hug.

"I can't believe we won Album of the Year! I can't believe we won Album of the Year!" she kept repeating. This was a big deal. Neither of us had won that award before.

"I just want to thank God," I remarked during my brief acceptance speech. "I want to thank Whitney Houston—she's the greatest. We all know that and loved that about her from the very beginning. I want to thank my family. I want to thank my studio and all the people who have helped me: Guru Sri Chinmoy and David Frazer, my engineer . . ."

Once again, in my nervousness as well as my haste to make way for my fellow producers to say their thank-yous, I forgot to acknowledge Clive Davis. After David Foster remembered to do this, so did several others, including Whitney. *Damn!* Brother Clive, I am *so sorry.* You really deserve the highest praise for having pulled the whole thing together.

When meeting the press backstage after the show, Nippy was still ecstatic, and her mood was infectious. We were *all* on a high, and this carried over to the postshow party where, together with Bobby, Robyn, and various other relatives, friends, and colleagues, we celebrated our success into the early morning hours. It was another unforgettable occasion, but afterward Whitney and I really didn't see a whole lot of each other.

At the time, my life had been going through some Major League changes: not least, my recent divorce from Anukampa and move to a new home. As one of Whitney's friends, Anukampa normally would have been the one to give her a call; without her around, that didn't happen. It was, therefore, a really nice surprise when, just before the 1994 Christmas holidays, my phone rang, I answered it, and Nippy's gentle voice was at the other end.

"Narada."

"Yeah?"

"It's *Whitney*!"

"Whitney?"

"Yeah! I was just thinking about you and wanted to see how you're doing."

"Wow, I'm so happy to hear from you! I'm shocked that you're calling."

"How *are* you?"

"I'm *good*! I *miss* you!"

"I miss you, too!"

"Well, when am I gonna see you?"

"Whenever you want! We can get together sometime."

"Great, great. So, what are *you* doing?"

"Oh, I'm just touring and raising my girl . . ."

The talk was easygoing—a warm chat between old friends— and I was truly touched that, out of the blue, while spending some precious home time with her husband and baby daughter, Whitney had thought of calling me.

In 1995, Nippy co-starred in *Waiting to Exhale* with Angela Bassett, Lela Rochon, and Loretta Devine. Babyface wrote and produced her songs on the soundtrack. Then, for the gospel album tied to the following year's remake of *The Preacher's Wife*, in which Whitney starred alongside Denzel Washington and Courtney B. Vance, she co-produced the songs with Mervyn Warren, Babyface, David Foster, Steve Lipson, and Rickey Minor. I never got the call, and the same applied to her next studio album, *My Love Is Your Love* (1998), which utilized the talents of ten different producers, just not me.

I didn't have a problem with this. Trends change, and life moves on. Seven of my productions appeared on Nippy's 2000 *Greatest Hits* compilation and four of them made their way onto the following year's *Love, Whitney* collection of ballads. However, my time working with her had clearly passed, and occupied with other production, composition, and drumming assignments, I could rest easy knowing that I had collaborated with one of the greatest popular singers of all time during her peak years. No one can ask for more than that.

In 2002, Whitney granted an interview to ABC's Diane Sawyer in which she discussed her volatile relationship with husband Bobby Brown, to whom she'd been married for the past decade. The topics included her sex, drugs, and rock 'n' roll lifestyle—with her famously admitting "the biggest devil is me"—and the $100 million lawsuit that had been filed against her by her father's company, John Houston Entertainment, for unpaid management fees. By then, John and Cissy had divorced, and Whitney began crying when Sawyer asked her how she felt about her dad. (John died at the age of eighty-two in February 2003, and the lawsuit was dismissed the following year.)

In the same interview, Whitney also mentioned that she and Robyn Crawford had fallen out a couple of years earlier due to Robyn arguing with Bobby as to who should be Nippy's adviser. As a result, the people I now had to deal with when trying to contact her were usually her sisters-in-law: Pat Houston, married to

Whitney's half-brother, Gary, and Donna Houston, married to her brother, Michael.

"I'd really like to come to Atlanta to spend a little time with her," I might tell Pat, referring to the city that became Whitney's home base in 2000.

"Okay, I'll ask her," I'd be assured, but I would never hear back. Calling Donna, I'd say, "This is Narada Michael Walden. I worked with Nippy on so many of her biggest hits."

"Oh, yes. Hi, Narada!"

"Can I just come and sit with her? I'll bring some songs, and if she likes any of them, we can get a little thing going."

"That sounds like a good idea!"

"Can you help make it happen?"

"I'll have a talk with her. She's been very busy."

Again, nothing. Eventually, I gave up.

The years passed and there wasn't much contact between Whitney and me. Mostly I would see her at industry events like Clive's pre-Grammy parties—looking a little older, but still beautiful—where we would always have a brief but friendly chat.

"How ya doin'?" I'd ask her.

"Doin' great!"

"What are you up to?"

"Oh, this and that . . ."

It was small talk, but the warmth of her smile and the caring tone in her voice reassured me that the love between us was still there even if the ongoing communication wasn't. Like everyone else, I had obviously heard about Whitney's personal problems and struggles with addiction. However, since I myself had never seen her acting high, it was hard to know precisely *what* was going on behind the scenes. I certainly never asked anyone close to her. I could only go by what I witnessed firsthand, and when I ran into her at Clive's February 2009 pre-Grammy party, she looked healthy if a little fuller-figured than before, her speaking voice sounded fine, and she appeared overjoyed to see me, jumping into my arms.

"Narada, please, let's get together. I want to talk to you. Give me a call."

Okay, that was a little different than the usual chitchat. About an hour later, I passed by the table where she was sitting. "We must get together," she repeated. "I want to record 'Lovin' Is Really My Game.'"

"I don't know that song," I replied.

"You *must* know it! It was a big disco hit for Brainstorm back in the late seventies."

"I really don't *know* it."

"Then *learn* it and cut it for me! I'll call you."

Able to get a copy of the 1978 single after returning to California, I immediately cut the track at Tarpan: a sub-eight-minute anthem with peaks, valleys, and endless string lines—hardcore funk and *real* disco. Whereas the hook—"Lovin' is really my game," repeated several times—was only sung twice on the original record, my rearrangement made sure this would happen more often on Whitney's version, emphasizing the hook to help it become a hit. Still, I'm sure it was the lyrics that caught her attention: "Why not give me a chance. I swear I could prove it, that don't mean I can't move it . . ." It was as if, after a lot of negative publicity and concern about drink-and-drug-induced damage being done to her voice, she was saying, "I'll show you I'm as good as I used to be."

I must have spent a week working on that track with my engineers David Frazer, Jim Reitzel, and Joe-L Angelo Margolis, as well as a number of musicians. But, after I sent Whitney a copy in Atlanta in March '09, I never heard back from her. I then called and left several messages with Pat Houston while being respectfully told, "She isn't available right now." Again, I didn't hear a thing—not even after my attorney tried to make things more businesslike by calling on my behalf.

A year later, in February 2010, I once more ran into Nippy at Clive's pre-Grammy party.

"Hey, Narada, we've got to do that *song*! 'Lovin' Is Really My Game.'"

Either she'd completely forgotten that I had sent it to her, or she had never been alerted to this. Then again, there could have been a general feeling that Whitney was in no fit shape to sing, certain people may not have liked the song, or there may have even been reluctance in some quarters for Nippy to work with me. These are just possibilities that I'm throwing out here; I myself don't have a clue. All I know is, she looked happy to see me and sounded genuine when asking me to cut the track. Had she heard it, she probably would have suggested we go record her vocal.

Thinking fast while instinctively not wishing to cause any trouble—when maybe I should have—I said that the track was ready but didn't mention I'd already sent it to her. "I'll get it to you by the start of next week," I added, and that is what I attempted to do. Once more, I heard nothing. Finally, I called Robyn and left a message. Within a day or so, she got back to me.

"Narada, if you love Whitney, pray for her."

"Of course I love Whitney."

"I know you do. You're a spiritual person, and you've always been good to her. So, please just pray for her."

"I will. But what's going on?"

"I don't want to go into it right now. I haven't been close to Whitney for quite some time, but we all need to pray for her."

That was a short and very *strange* conversation. However, if Robyn Crawford was now asking me to pray for Whitney Houston, *something* was up.

At this point, trying to get in touch with Nippy was clearly a waste of time. And, as things turned out, I'd only get to see and talk with her one more time: predictably, at Clive's February 2011 pre-Grammy gala. After I arrived, the first person I ran into was Dionne Warwick. I told her—not for the first time—how much I loved her and how much she had influenced me. Then she asked, "Did you say hi to Whitney?"

"No, where is she?"

"She's sitting right over there."

The two of us approached the table where Nippy was with Cissy and Bobbi Kristina who, now nearly seventeen, bore a strong resemblance to her dad. When Whitney saw me she was much more subdued than usual. Normally, she'd jump up, give me a hug, and act all excited, but not this time. While Cissy, Bobbi, Dionne, and a bunch of other people engaged in conversation, Whitney was very sweet and very calm—looking good but lower energy.

"I still want to do that song," she said quietly.

"Honey, I've *got* that song."

"'Lovin' Is Really My Game'?"

"*Yeah!* Can we go do it?"

"Okay. I'll give you a call."

Bobbi had apparently been eavesdropping on our conversation.

"Mama, tell him *I* wanna sing," she eagerly interjected, putting an arm around Nippy's shoulder while looking at her with wide eyes. It seemed like they had already talked about the possibility of Bobbi following in her mom's footsteps.

"Whatever your mama wants," I responded, while trying to observe Whitney's reaction. This amounted to a gentle smile and knowing look, as if to say, *I've been down that road and I know how hard it is to be a singer. I'm not sure if I want to curse you with that just yet.*

Message received. I wasn't going to play along with Bobbi if her mom was in any way undecided as to what she should do. Returning to "Lovin' Is Really My Game," I told Nippy, "I've got the song. We can do it. Let's go."

"Okay. Love you, love you, love you!"

She blew me some kisses, and that was that.

Again I had my assistant send the recording, *again* I tried following up—calling Gary Houston, who referred me to Pat, since Donna was no longer around—and *again* I got nowhere. On March 24, I finally gave Clive a call.

"Clive, it's Narada. How are you?"

"Doing fine. It's good to hear from you, Narada! We've worked together on so many great hit records."

As always, Clive was very nice, very respectful. After discussing a song that Aretha was interested in recording, I came straight to the point: "I'd love to work with Whitney again. Is there any way we can shake things up and make that happen?"

"Not unless she goes back into rehab," came the reply.

That clarified the situation. For now, at least, working with Nippy was a no-go.

===⬩===

IT WAS SATURDAY, FEBRUARY 11, 2012. Burned out from two years of touring the world as Jeff Beck's drummer, I'd decided to drive up the California coast with my significant other, Katie—instead of south to attend the next day's Grammy Awards—and take a short break in Gualala, about three hours north of San Francisco. Our cabin, located on a stretch of remote coast overlooking the Pacific Ocean, had no TV or radio, but I happened to have a small AM transistor radio in my travel bag. Late that afternoon, I asked Katie to hand it to me while I relaxed in a huge bathtub of hot water.

"I Wanna Dance with Somebody" was playing on the only station my little radio could tune into. *Cool,* I thought, closing my eyes. Then, as the song ended, the deejay cut in: "I don't know why Whitney Houston recorded *that.* It's not very good . . . Anyway, she died today."

I lay in the bath, completely stunned. Then another song played—my brain didn't register which one—and an even terser announcement followed: "Yeah, well, she's dead." No respect, no nothing. My shock turned to anger. Only several minutes later did that sonofabitch add the detail that she had died in a bathtub. *Synchronicity, my darling Baby Nippy, synchronicity.*

Throughout the night, Katie and I were glued to that little radio for updates about the events leading up to Whitney's death. The partying, the pills, the erratic behavior—by the early morning hours, I reached a saturation point where I thought, *Enough!* Before her body was even cold all of these so-called experts were tearing it apart. What about all of the good times? What about all of the love and happiness? What about all of the incredible music?

In between the news bulletins, I was comforted by Nippy's songs and the sound of her beautiful voice. Still, how could someone so vibrant, so charismatic, so *alive* suddenly be gone? Nippy's presence was *huge*, enough to fill any stadium, and without her around there was an empty space in this world. There was also pain in my heart, and I felt sick to my stomach, yet her spirit was all around us. Katie and I both felt it—warm, upbeat, enveloping our souls.

It's your time to shine, it's your time.

These are the words that began crystallizing in Katie's mind as the sun rose in a clear blue sky—the first new day without our Whitney on this Earth.

Every rock, mountain, and tree
radiates your energy and beauty.
Your love surrounds me.

WE DROVE SLOWLY DOWN the coast road—thinking, reflecting, reminiscing. Then, once we arrived home, I felt compelled to reach out to Cissy. No way could I even imagine what she must have been feeling. But, for what it was worth, I wanted to share my own feelings with her and let her know how Nippy had touched my life.

Dear Cissy,

I'm very saddened and at the same time I'm so proud of my Whitney Houston. She gave us her all. I'm so proud of the great music we worked on together. She was my sister, my friend, and one of the greatest singers and women I have ever known. My heart goes out to her, knowing she didn't have to suffer. My heart goes out to all of us who know she truly loved us. My heart especially goes out to her beautiful daughter Bobbi who I spoke with at this same time last year . . . God, thank you for sharing Whitney our angel with us even for a short while. She really did open up our hearts and bring in Your Heavenly sunlight.

Cissy, my love goes out to you . . . Sympathies to you and the close family. Blessings, love, and gratitude to you, Darling Whitney.

With love eternally,
Your Narada

Heartbreak doesn't begin to describe what I was feeling—heartbreak over the premature extinguishing of such a bright, vibrant flame in all of our lives; heartbreak over what might have been and what would never be; heartbreak over *our* loss, not Whitney's, since she, thankfully, was now at peace.

DURING THE NEXT FEW DAYS, inundated with media requests for my thoughts, feelings, and recollections about Nippy, I appeared on radio and TV to celebrate her life amid a torrent of gossip and speculation about the circumstances surrounding her death. As I told CNN's Piers Morgan before going on air, "I want to talk about Whitney's music and promote her inspirational genius." To his credit, having already discussed her problems with previous guests, he was happy to go along with this, and the same applied to everyone else who interviewed me.

A week later, I attended the funeral service with my mom at Newark's New Hope Baptist Church. The fifteen hundred guests included everyone from Oprah Winfrey, Spike Lee, and the

Reverend Jesse Jackson to Chaka Khan, Jennifer Hudson, Queen Latifah, and Mariah Carey. Clive Davis arranged the whole event.

The program commenced with singing by the choir that was so uplifting, I could feel Whitney's spirit bopping around the room. Introduced by Dionne, Alicia Keys performed "Send Me an Angel," Stevie Wonder sang "Ribbon in the Sky," CeCe Winans performed "Don't Cry for Me," and BeBe added to the supercharged atmosphere with a moving rendition of "I Really Miss You."

Pat Houston talked about Whitney's love of God, Kevin Costner spoke touchingly about working with her on *The Bodyguard*, Rickey Minor recalled crafting the musical arrangement for her unforgettable Super Bowl rendition of the "Star-Spangled Banner," and the Reverend Marvin Winans delivered a powerful eulogy to close the service.

> Father, we thank you for this life of Whitney Elizabeth "Nippy" Houston. We thank you that she was a dear friend, and we echo the sentiments of all that have come to show their love. Father, I pray, by the power of the Holy Spirit, that you would give all that are under the sound of my voice the thought to prioritize, to make you first, for us not to talk about you, but for us to live for you.

> Let us leave here recognizing that Whitney left too soon. Let us leave here impacted by her life, saying that I want to finish what God has started. Let us make you first. I pray that you will lift up Mike and Gary and Pat and Bobbi Kristina, lift up Cissy, lift up Aunt Bay, lift up Dionne, all of those that are touched, all of us that are hurting—that you would lift us up. And Father, we will not leave here bitter or upset.

Singing, Reverend Winans concluded: *But let the church say amen. Let the church say amen. God has spoken, so let the church say amen.*

Walking outside with tears still running down my face, looking at Nippy's thousands of fans and nearly as many representatives from the media, I heard in my mind the speech I would have given . . .

Those who knew Whitney Houston know all about her incredible charge of electricity. She turned the light on. Before Whitney came along, none of us ever saw a light like hers. I've worked with a lot of great people, but Nippy's charm and effervescence generated a unique kind of energy.

Here was something new that we weren't yet hip to, a physical and spiritual hybrid that we'd never seen before. We had to slow down our breathing just to take it all in, to do this spirit justice, and let it take over. I never knew anyone with her level of confidence, her vocal genius, or her inner and outer beauty. Encountering all of this at the same time, it was hard not to be scared, intimidated, and just plain bowled over. That's why we had to breathe slowly, open ourselves up, and welcome it all in.

Being with Whitney was always an eye-opening experience. I'd think I knew her, but she would keep growing and keep evolving. She grew so fast, and what she wanted to achieve for herself became both higher and deeper. At the same time, she was so confident. She loved her voice, loved what she did. Working with her was always enjoyable, and when God walked through the room, we were able to capture her spirit and get it down on tape.

We can't measure Whitney's legacy as an artist anymore than we can measure the universe. However, being a Leo, she was a heart person, and we could hear and feel that whenever she sang to us. She saw her mom perform that way, and she was raised in church that way, surrounded by all that spirit, jubilation, and celebration. That's where she came from and that's what we felt when she sang to us—all that warmth, all that hospitality, all that genuine care. Her energy and fire and passion for life were so unbelievable, I want the whole world to know she was the real deal.

Whitney's wasn't a life wasted. Her voice was otherworldly, her body of work was phenomenal, and both will live for all time. So, let's celebrate her life. It is God's hour for her to go home now, and while it's all right for us to cry and mourn her passing, we must also let her rest. God bless you, our beloved Nippy.

THE BEAUTY OF
WHAT YOU DO

T WAS EARLY 1990, the place was New York City's Right Track Recording, and Whitney and I were hanging out in the main studio area after she'd just finished tracking her vocal for "All the Man That I Need." Some personal issues had made the past week less than easy for her, but Nippy's resilience and indomitable spirit, combined with my patience and understanding, had helped her weather the storm, and now she was emerging into the sunlight.

"You know, people don't have any idea how much hard work goes into making these songs, making these records," she remarked in a voice so soft it barely rose above a whisper.

"You're right. They don't have a clue."

"Sometimes, I myself don't even know what I'm going to sing."

"Yeah, but that's the beauty of what you do. You're always surprising me, and you're always surprising yourself."

"Aw, no, you're so sweet . . . I mean, look at that guy over there behind the console. Look at how many buttons he has to push to make all of this happen."

"Well, quite honestly, Whitney, the engineers never get any respect."

"That's *true*. I don't like that."

"You know what we should do? We should have a dinner, a big banquet, for all the engineers everywhere."

"I like *that*!"

"Then why don't we do that? You can host it. You're big enough now."

"Okay, Narada, let's do it."

"Are you feeling better?"

"Yeah. It was really hard for awhile, but I'm feeling much better now."

"Good, because I want you to know I love you and I'm here for you."

"I know that. I know that. I know that."

"Are you sure you know that?"

"I *know* that."

ACKNOWLEDGMENTS

WISH TO THANK THE following people for their inspiration, love, and involvement in my life during the years covered by this book:

The Houstons—Cissy, John, Gary, Mike, Donna, Pat, and Whitney's entire family.

Clive Davis, for choosing me to be Whitney's producer.

My mother, Peggy; father, Harold; and brother, Kevin Walden.

My first wife, Anukampa Lisa Walden, and girlfriend, Katie Merserau.

My Tarpan team and other invaluable sources of help—Kimrea, Jim Reitzel, Joe-L Angelo Margolis, James Donnelly, Janice Lee, Shiloh Hobel, Cherise Miller, Lulu Holmgren, Mariana Rosmis, Corinne Afanasieff, Junko Kawai, Mckenzie Earley, Lisa Petrides, Kelly McRae, Stefani Shaffer, Liz Jackson, Sally Gerharter, Sandie Van Fleet, and Beverly Green.

Recording engineers David Frazer, Lincoln Clapp, Michael Barbiero, Dana Jon Chappelle, Matt Rohr, Marc "Elvis" Reyburn,

Bob Rosa, Maureen Droney, Ken Kessie, Fernando Kral, Gordon Lyon, and Jay Rifkin.

All of the singers, musicians, and arrangers who contributed so beautifully to Whitney's records, including Walter Afanasieff, Kitty Beethoven, Vernon "Ice" Black, Bongo Bob Smith, Kevin Dorsey, Aretha Franklin, Kenny G, Michael Gibbs, Jim Gilstrap, Preston Glass, Greg "Gigi" Gonaway, Jennifer Hall, Jerry Hey, Niki Haris, Randy Jackson, Ren Klyce, Paul Leim, Cory Lerios, Frank Martin, Myrna Matthews, Raul Rekow, Claytoven Richardson, Marc Russo, Corrado Rustici, Doc Shafer, Sterling, Premik Russell Tubbs, Shambhu Neil Vineberg, Wayne Wallace, and anyone else I've forgotten to mention!

Sting, Carlos Santana, and Quincy Jones for their kind words.

Chaka Khan for her fabulous foreword.

Don Lemon and Piers Morgan at CNN.

Gerry Griffith, Donnie Lenner, and Roy Lott at Arista Records; my managers Greg DiGiovine and David Rubinson; and my attorney Barry Platnick.

Whitney's dear friend Robyn Crawford.

Guru Sri Chinmoy and Alo Devi, along with my fellow disciples Apeksha, Ashrita, and Mahavishnu John McLaughlin.

My colleagues at the Narada Michael Walden Foundation.

Raoul Goff, Michael Madden, Roxanna Aliaga, Robbie Schmidt, Chrissy Kwasnik, Elizabeth Dougherty, and everyone at Insight Editions.

My co-author Richard Buskin and his life partner, Marci Santora-Shontz. Big love to you, Richard, for putting together my first book so brilliantly.

And last but not least, Whitney's fans. My love to you all for sustaining her divine spirit.

Long live Whitney Nippy Houston!

APPENDIX

Whitney Houston Recordings Produced by Narada Michael Walden

Track	Peak Chart Position						
Songs listed in the order they were recorded	US	UK	AUS	AUT	CAN	FRA	GER
"How Will I Know" (George Merrill, Shannon Rubicam, Narada Michael Walden)	1	5	2	28	1	111	26
"For the Love of You" (Isley Brothers, Chris Jasper)	-	-	-	-	-	-	-
"I Wanna Dance with Somebody (Who Loves Me)"* (George Merrill, Shannon Rubicam)	1	1	1	1	1	3	1
"Just the Lonely Talking Again" (Sam Dees)	-	-	-	-	-	-	-
"I Know Him So Well" (Tim Rice, Benny Andersson, Björn Ulvaeus)	-	-	-	-	-	-	46
"Where Do Broken Hearts Go" (Frank Wildhorn, Chuck Jackson)	1	14	48	-	6	-	-
"Love Is a Contact Sport" (Preston Glass)	-	-	-	-	-	-	-
"So Emotional" (Billy Steinberg, Tom Kelly)	1	5	26	-	9	21	-

* "I Wanna Dance with Somebody (Who Loves Me)" was also number one in
  Belgium, Finland, Italy, New Zealand, Norway, and South Africa.

NLD	SWE	SWI	US Single Release Date	Album/Single
15	2	11	November 22, 1985	*Whitney Houston*
-	-	-		*Whitney*
15	1	1	April 30, 1987	*Whitney*
-	-	-		*Whitney*
14	-	-		*Whitney*
47	-	-	February 25, 1988	*Whitney*
-	-	-		*Whitney*
23	-	30	November 12, 1987	*Whitney*

Track	Peak Chart Position						
Songs listed in the order they were recorded	US	UK	AUS	AUT	CAN	FRA	GER
"Moment of Truth" (Jan Buckingham, David Paul Bryant)	-	-	-	-	-	-	-
"One Moment in Time" (Albert Hammond, John Bettis)	5	1	49	5	3	8	1
"It Isn't, It Wasn't, It Ain't Never Gonna Be" (Albert Hammond, Diane Warren)	41	29	-	-	43	-	-
"Feels So Good" (Bryan Loren)	-	-	-	-	-	-	-
"I Belong to You" (Franne Golde, Derek Bramble)	-	54	-	-	-	-	-
"All the Man That I Need" (Dean Pitchford, Michael Gore)	1	13	63	21	1	28	37
"Dancin' on the Smooth Edge" (David Lasley, Robbie Long)	-	-	-	-	-	-	-
"Higher Love" (Steve Winwood, Will Jennings)	-	-	-	-	-	-	-
"Lover for Life" (Sam Dees)	-	-	-	-	-	-	-
"I'm Every Woman" (Nickolas Ashford, Valerie Simpson)	4	4	11	19	2	11	13
"Look Into Your Heart" (Curtis Mayfield)	-	-	-	-	-	-	-

NLD	SWE	SWI	US Single Release Date	Album/Single
-	-	-		B side of "I Wanna Dance with Somebody"
6	3	4	August 27, 1988	*1988 Summer Olympics Album*
40	-	-	July 17, 1989	*Through the Storm* [Aretha Franklin album]
-	-	-		B side of "I'm Your Baby Tonight" maxi-single
79	-	-	October 18, 1991	*I'm Your Baby Tonight*
9	-	28	December 4, 1990	*I'm Your Baby Tonight*
-	-	-		B side of "All the Man That I Need"
-	-	-		Bonus track on Japanese release of *I'm Your Baby Tonight*
-	-	-		*I'm Your Baby Tonight*
3	7	18	January 2, 1993	*The Bodyguard: Original Soundtrack Album*
-	-	-		*A Tribute to Curtis Mayfield*

INSIGHT EDITIONS

PO Box 3088
San Rafael, CA 94912

www.INSIGHTEDITIONS.com
FOR WEB EXCLUSIVE CONTENT!

Find us on Facebook: www.facebook.com/InsightEditions

Follow us on Twitter: @insighteditions

Library of Congress Cataloging-in-Publication Data available.
ISBN: 978-1-60887-200-8

COLOPHON
Publisher—Raoul Goff
Art Director—Christine Kwasnik
Designer—Jon Glick
Acquiring Editors—Robbie Schmidt and Michael Madden
Editor—Roxanna Aliaga
Production Manager—Anna Wan
Additional editorial work by Jan Hughes, and design and production support by Jenelle Wagner,
Jane Chinn, and Binh Matthews.

Insight Editions would especially like to thank Narada Michael Walden, Richard Buskin, Kimrea,
Chaka Khan, Quincy Jones, Carlos Santana, and Sting.

ROOTS of PEACE   REPLANTED PAPER   Insight Editions, in association with Roots of Peace, will plant two trees
for each tree used in the manufacturing of this book. Roots of Peace is an internationally renowned
humanitarian organization dedicated to eradicating land mines worldwide and converting war-torn lands
into productive farms and wildlife habitats. Roots of Peace will plant two million fruit and nut trees in
Afghanistan and provide farmers there with the skills and support necessary for sustainable land use.

Manufactured in the United States by Insight Editions

10 9 8 7 6 5 4 3 2 1